Liberalism

Concepts in Social Thought

Series Editor: Frank Parkin
Magdalen College, Oxford

Liberalism   *John Gray*

Ideology   *David McLellan*

Conservatism   *Robert Nisbet*

Concepts in Social Thought

Liberalism

John Gray

University of Minnesota Press

Minneapolis

Published by the University of Minnesota Press
2037 University Avenue southeast, Minneapolis
MN 55414.
Published simultaneously in Canada
by Fitzhenry & Whiteside Limited, Markham.
Printed in Great Britain

Library of Congress Cataloging-in-Publication Data
Gray, John
   Liberalism
   (Concepts in social thought)
   86–1411

ISBN 0–8166–1520–9

ISBN 0–8166–1521–7 (pbk.)

The University of Minnesota
is an equal-opportunity
educator and employer.

Contents

Preface and Acknowledgements

In this short book I aim to give an account of liberalism – what it is, whence it came and what might still be hoped for it. I write as a liberal. I do not pretend that my inquiry occupies any space of moral or political neutrality. At the same time, I hope my account shows an awareness of the limits and difficulties of liberalism, and I would like this book to be useful to critics of liberalism as well as to its friends. I have not aimed to add to the growing number of contemporary studies in liberal social philosophy, since I intend to do that on another occasion. Instead I have tried to show what it means to be a liberal, and why the liberal outlook remains compelling today.

The first phase of serious work on this book was done during a period of residence as Distinguished Research Fellow in the Center for Social Philosophy and Policy at Bowling Green State University in Ohio. I wish to thank the directors of the Center, and in particular Jeffrey Paul and Fred Miller, for their support of my work on this book. I completed the book during my stay as Visiting Professor in the Department of Philosophy at Bowling Green State University, and I wish to thank the Chair of the Department, Tom Attig, for his many kindnesses and assistance, and Pat Bressler for arranging the typing of my (sometimes barely decipherable) manuscript.

For encouraging me to press on with my work on liberalism, I am indebted to David H. Padden of the Cato Institute in Washington, D.C. For his detailed comments on a draft of the first half of the book, I wish to thank Douglas

Den Uyl. For conversation on the central themes of this book, and comments on its early chapters, I am grateful to Neera Badhwar.

Notwithstanding these acknowledgements, all the usual disclaimers apply. Responsibility for the book remains mine alone.

John Gray
Jesus College, Oxford

Introduction: The Unity of the Liberal Tradition

Though historians have uncovered elements of the liberal outlook in the ancient world, and most particularly in classical Greece and Rome, these elements form part of the prehistory of liberalism rather than components of the modern liberal movement. As a political current and an intellectual tradition, an identifiable strand in thought and practice, liberalism is no older than the seventeenth century. The epithet 'liberal' is used of a political movement for the first time, indeed, only in the nineteenth century, when in 1812 it was adopted by the Spanish party of Liberales. Before that date, the system of thought of classical liberalism had been raised up, above all in the period of the Scottish Enlightenment, when Adam Smith referred to 'the liberal plan of equality, liberty and justice', but the term 'liberal' still functioned chiefly as a derivative of liberality, the classical virtue of humanity, generosity and the open mind. Essential to any correct understanding of liberalism, accordingly, is a clear insight into its historicity, its origins in a definite cultural and political circumstance and its background in the context of European individualism in the early modern period. For, whereas liberalism has no single, unchanging nature or essence, it has a set of distinctive features which exhibits its modernity and at the same time marks it off from other modern intellectual traditions and their associated political movements. These features are all of them fully intelligible only in the historical perspective given by the several crises of modernity – the dissolution of the feudal order in Europe in the sixteenth and seventeenth

centuries, the events surrounding the French and American
Revolutions in the last decade of the eighteenth century, the
emergence of democratic and socialist mass movements during the second half of the nineteenth century and the near-
eclipse of liberal society by totalitarian governments in our
own times. In this way, the distinctive features which marked
the liberal conception of man and society at its inception in
seventeenth-century England were altered and reshaped, but
not changed out of recognition, as the individualist societies
which had given birth to liberal ideas were subject to renewed
and different challenges.

Common to all variants of the liberal tradition is a definite
conception, distinctively modern in character, of man and
society. What are the several elements of this conception? It
is *individualist*, in that it asserts the moral primacy of the person against the claims of any social collectivity; *egalitarian*,
inasmuch as it confers on all men the same moral status and
denies the relevance to legal or political order of differences
in moral worth among human beings; *universalist*, affirming
the moral unity of the human species and according a secon-
dary importance to specific historic associations and cultural
forms; and *meliorist* in its affirmation of the corrigibility and
improvability of all social institutions and political arrangements. It is this conception of man and society which gives
liberalism a definite identity which transcends its vast internal
variety and complexity. To be sure, this liberal conception has
several distinct and even conflicting sources in European
culture, and it has been given concrete historical embodiment
in diverse ways. It owes something to Stoicism and to Christianity, it has been inspired by scepticism and by a fideistic
certainty of divine revelation and it has exalted the power of
reason even as, in other contexts, it has sought to humble
reason's claims. Again, the liberal tradition has sought valid-
ation or justification in very different philosophies. Liberal
moral and political claims have been grounded in theories of
the natural rights of man as often as they have been defended
by appeal to a utilitarian theory of conduct, and they have
sought support from both science and religion. Finally,
like any other current of opinion, liberalism has acquired a
different flavor in each of the different national cultures in

which it has had a persistent life. Throughout its history French liberalism has been notably different from liberalism in England, liberalism in Germany has always confronted unique problems and American liberalism, though much indebted to English and French thought and practice, soon acquired novel features of its own. At times, it must seem to the historian of ideas and movements that there is not one liberalism, but rather many, linked together only by a loose family resemblance.

For all the rich historical diversity which liberalism yields to historical investigation, it is none the less a mistake to suppose that the manifold varieties of liberalism cannot be understood as variations on a small set of distinctive themes. Liberalism constitutes a single tradition, rather than two or more traditions or a diffuse syndrome of ideas, precisely in virtue of the four elements composing the liberal conception of man and society which were earlier sketched. These elements are refined and redefined, their mutual relations ordered anew and their content enriched at several phases in the history of the liberal tradition and in a variety of national and cultural contexts in which they are often given a highly specific interpretation. For all its historical variability, liberalism remains an integral outlook, whose principal components are not hard to specify, rather than a loose association of movements and outlooks among which family resemblances may be described. It is only thus that we can identify John Locke and Immanuel Kant, John Stuart Mill and Herbert Spencer, J. M. Keynes and F. A. Hayek, John Rawls and Robert Nozick as embodying separate branches of a common lineage. The character of liberalism as a single tradition, its identity as a persistent though variable conception of man and society, holds true even if, as shall later be suggested, it has been subject to a major rupture, when in the writings of John Stuart Mill classical liberalism gave way to the modern or revisionist liberalism of our own times.

PART ONE: HISTORICAL

1

The Pre-modern Anticipations of Liberalism

According to the great eighteenth century French liberal writer, Benjamin Constant, the ancient world had a conception of liberty radically different from that held in modern times. Whereas, for modern men, liberty signifies a protected sphere of non-interference or independence under the rule of law, for the ancients it meant entitlement to a voice in collective decision-making. It was this ancient view of liberty, according to Constant, that J. J. Rousseau sought anachronistically to revive when he glorified the disciplined life of Sparta. How valid or useful is this distinction of Constant's? It marks an important insight insofar as it affirms that the dominant idea of freedom among the ancient Greeks was not the idea of an assured space of individual independence. For the Greeks, as perhaps for the Romans, the idea of freedom was applied as naturally to communities – where it meant self-rule, or the absence of external control – as it was to individuals. Even in its applications to individuals, it rarely connoted any immunity from control by the community, but only an entitlement to participation in its deliberations. The ancient idea of freedom is so far in sharp contrast with the modern one.

At the same time, Constant's insight is easily exaggerated and its essential soundness should not lead us to neglect the germs of liberal ideas among the ancients, and particularly

among the Greeks. Especially noteworthy among the Greeks
are the Sophists, sceptical thinkers who, in making a sharp
distinction between the natural and the conventional, tended
to assert the universal equality of men. So it is that Glaucon,
in the second book of Plato's *Republic,* develops a theory of
social contract which has plainly a Sophistic origin. 'Justice'
he says 'is a contract neither to do nor to suffer wrong'. Again,
Lycophron the Sophist is cited by Aristotle as holding that law
and the state depend on a contract, such that the only end of
the law is the security of the individual and the functions of the
state are all negative functions having to do with the prevention of injustice. The special force of the Sophistic distinction
between nature and convention was, of course, to reject the
idea of natural slavery. The rhetorician Alcidamas is reported
to have asserted that: 'The gods made all men free; nature
made none a slave.'

Finally, it was by the Sophists that a doctrine of political
equality was first developed against the esoteric and élitist
conceptions of government until then current among the
Greeks. As G. B. Kerferd observes: 'The importance of this
doctrine of Protagoras (of political equality) in the history of
political thought can hardly be exaggerated.' He goes on:
'Protagoras produced for the first time in human history a
theoretical basis for participatory democracy' – the basis
being Protagoras' doctrine that all men have a share (though
not the same share) in justice.[1]

In the same generation as Lycophron and Alcidamas – the
generation which K. R. Popper calls the Great Generation,
and which lived in Athens just before and during the Pelopon-
nesian War – Pericles gave in his famous *Funeral Oration* a
statement of liberal egalitarian and individualist principles.
Though their domain of application was implicitly restricted
by him to Greeks, and even, perhaps, only to Athenians, his
speech was pregnant with significance for the later development of the liberal tradition. Of the Athenian democracy he
says:

> The laws afford equal justice to all alike in their private dis-
> putes, but we do not ignore the claims of excellence . . . . The
> freedom we enjoy extends also to ordinary life; we are not
> suspicious of one another, and do not nag our neighbour if he

chooses to go his own way . . . . But this freedom does not make us lawless. We are taught to respect the magistrates and the laws, and never to forget that we must protect the injured . . . . We are free to live exactly as we please, and yet, we are always ready to face any danger.

It is in Pericles, perhaps, that we find the clearest statement of the liberal outlook which joined together the Great Generation and which encompasses the schools of the Sophists, Protagoras and Gorgias, and of Democritus the atomist.

In the works of Plato and Aristotle, we find, not the further development of the liberal outlook of the Great Generation, but instead a reaction against it – an emasculation of Greek liberalism,[2] or a counter-revolution against the open society of Periclean Athens.[3] In the works of Plato and his disciple, Aristotle, the sceptical and empirical outlook of the Sophists and of Democritus is replaced by a species of metaphysical rationalism, and the ethics of freedom and equality are repudiated, radically by Plato and more moderately, but no less consistently, by Aristotle. In the *Republic*, Plato advances what is, in effect, an anti-liberal Utopia. For in it the claims of individuality go unprotected and indeed unrecognized, moral equality among men is repudiated and, once established, social institutions are exempt from criticism and improvement. In his response to the germs of modern liberalism present in the teachings of the Sophists, Plato elaborated one of the most systematic and powerful attacks on the idea of human freedom to be found in intellectual history.

In Aristotle's thought the anti-liberal sentiment is not as virulent as that which animates Plato's works, but it remains strong and pervasive. Many historians of political thought go so far as to deny that any conception of individual freedom or human right may be found in Aristotle on the ground that ascribing any element of the liberal outlook to a pre-modern thinker involves anachronism, but this claim seems baseless, since there is clear evidence of modern individualist conceptions among the Sophists, as we have seen. Alasdair MacIntyre declares sweepingly that

> there is no expression in any ancient or medieval language correctly translated by our expression "a right" until near the

close of the Middle Ages. The concept lacks any means of expression in Hebrew, Greek, Latin or Arabic . . . or in Japanese as late as the mid-nineteenth century.[4]

In much the same view, Leo Strauss contrasts 'classic natural right' in the adjectival sense with modern theories of natural rights, claiming that ancient natural right is grounded in civic duty whereas modern natural rights theories assert an entitlement to individual liberty that holds independently of and prior to any civic obligation.[5] The truth in these large claims is that nowhere in Aristotle is there any glimmering of an assertion of the negative right to individual liberty postulated by such modernists as Hobbes and Locke and, in Aristotle's own day, by the Sophists. It may nevertheless be argued that Aristotle's ethics contain in rudimentary form some conception of natural human rights – rights, that is, to say, possessed by all human beings in virtue of their membership of the species. Such a conception is intimated at several points in the *Nicomachean Ethics,* as when it is claimed that the exercise of moral judgement involves the exercise of individual responsibility, and virtue is thereby connected with choice-making.[6] The natural rights hinted at in such passages are by no means the negative rights of modern liberalism, to be sure, and they coexist uneasily with Aristotle's muddled defence of natural slavery, but they remain affirmations of natural rights of a sort, most akin to the conception of natural rights as grounded in natural justice adumbrated in medieval times by Aquinas. To this extent, whereas MacIntyre is mistaken that ideas of natural right were unknown among the ancients, Strauss seems to be on firmer ground in arguing that the dominant idea of natural right among the ancients was duty-based. In Aristotle, indeed, it was almost a functional conception of rights as being claims generated by the different roles men perform in the *polis*. These functions were clearly conceived by Aristotle as yielding very unequal rights, without ever generating a right to noninterference or personal independence. Aristotle's consequent rejection of political equality must, in fact, be seen as part and parcel of his conservative reaction against the nascent liberalism of Athens. It is with Aristotle, in fact, that the proto-liberal period in Greek life closes, and we must turn to the Romans for the next significant episode in the pre-history of the liberal tradition.

Among the Romans, the Laws of the Twelve Tables, which may have been composed on the model of Solon's laws, embodied important guarantees of individual freedom. The first of the public laws they contain enjoins that 'no privileges or statutes shall be enacted in favor of private persons, to the injury of others contrary to the law common to all citizens and which individuals, no matter of what rank, have a right to make use of'. It was on this basis that there grew up in Rome a highly developed and in many ways strongly individualist private law. This individualistic legal tradition decayed in later times, especially under the rule of Justinian and Constantine, but it was influential in modern times through the medium of the Latin Renaissance of the seventeenth century. Especially significant in this connection are Livy, Tacitus and Cicero, historians and orators whose works embody in informal style the free spirit of Roman law in its individualist phase. Indeed, F. A. Hayek goes so far as to characterize Cicero as 'the main authority for modern liberalism'. 'To him' Hayek says 'is due the conception of general rules or *leges legum,* which govern legislation, the conception that we obey the law in order to be free, and the conception that the judge ought to be merely the mouth through which the law speaks.[7] Important, also, are a number of Stoic writers, especially the emperor Marcus Aurelius, who in their conception of the rational unity of the human species as conferred by participation in the divine *logos* anticipate the modern liberal ideal of universalism. But these Stoic contributions were perhaps less important for the future of liberalism than the achievement for a period of Roman history of an individualist legal order. In ancient Rome, then, as in classical Greece, some of the elements of the liberal outlook were present and, for a time, embodied in practice through the institutions of individualist law.

What of the contribution of Christianity to the liberal idea of freedom? According to a well-established historiographical tradition exemplified in the writings of Gibbon and Hume, the conversion of the Roman Empire to Christian faith in the reign of Constantine and thereafter represented the eclipse of ancient values of religious toleration and respect for learning and intelligence. On that view, Christianity brought about a triumph of barbarism and religion and inaugurated a dark age of intolerance and ignorance. As against this, there is little doubt that early Christianity was by comparison with the religions of the Romans and the Jews an individualist faith. Its concentration in the salvation of the individual and its affirmation of the imminent end of all things encouraged a loosening of the moral disciplines of the old religions and amounted to an intensification of the spirit of individuality expressed in many of the philosophies and religions of the late Roman period. Like the individualism of the Stoics and Epicureans, however, that of the early Christians was anti-political rather than proto-liberal. It neither had, nor was perceived to have, any definite implications for political order. Thus, once it had emancipated itself from its origins in Judaism, Christianity became a universal religion, doctrinally committed to a belief in the original equality of all souls. But this was a doctrine compatible with a broad variety of political arrangements.

For all these reasons, the moral inheritance of Christianity to the medieval and early modern periods was complex and even contradictory. While Christianity indeed brought an end to the ancient tradition of freedom of enquiry and comparative religious toleration, at the same time it transmitted to us the universalist and individualist outlook found in several of the religious and philosophical movements of the later Roman period. In preserving these achievements of Imperial Rome, Christianity passed on to modernity, in a form containing authentic elements of its own, one of the chief strands entering into the formation of the liberal tradition.

Liberalism in the Early Modern Period

It is in the seventeenth century that we find the first systematic expositions of the modern individualist outlook from which the liberal tradition springs. In England, Thomas Hobbes (1588–1679) gives voice to an intransigent individualism whose consummate modernity marks a decisive breach with the social philosophy bequeathed by Plato and Aristotle to medieval Christendom. In its general outlines, Hobbes's thought is familiar enough. From a hypothetical state of nature in which each man cannot avoid being at war with every other, Hobbes derives the artefact of civil association, which is a condition of peace secured by the unlimited authority of a coercive sovereign power. Hobbes's postulates about the human condition – his assertion that each man acts always with a view to his own benefit, his belief that men are compelled to avoid violent death as the greatest of evils and his insistence that most of the good things in life are inherently scarce – lead him to reject outright classical notions of the supreme good or final end of human life and the place that the classical conception of the *summum bonum* had in social philosophy. He conceives of political arrangements as artifices whereby men achieve a partial remedy for the natural evils of their lot rather than as providing the necessary conditions of human flourishing and virtue. Civil society, as assured by the authority of the sovereign, is a framework in which each man may pursue his restless striving for pre-eminence over his fellows without thereby inaugurating a disastrous war of all against all. The radical modernity of Hobbesian individualism is exhibited unmistakably in his repudiation of classical ideas about the natural end or final cause of human existence. Hobbes replaced the Aristotelian conception of human well being as a state of self-realization or flourishing by the claim that by their nature and circumstance men are unavoidably condemned to an incessant pursuit of the ever changing objects of their desires.

All these features of Hobbes's thought are familiar tokens of his modernity. Less familiar, though remarked upon by the greatest of Hobbes scholars, are his affinities with liberalism. His closeness to liberalism lies in part, of course, in his uncompromising individualism. It is found also, however, in his egalitarian affirmation of the equal liberty of all men in the state of nature and his firm rejection of a purely hereditary title to political authority. Leo Strauss puts the case for Hobbes as the chief progenitor of liberalism as follows:

> If, then, natural law must be deduced from the desire for self-preservation, if, in other words, the desire for self-preservation is the root of all justice and morality, the fundamental moral fact is not a duty but a right; all duties are derivative from the fundamental and inalienable right of self-preservation. There are, then, no absolute or unconditional duties; duties are binding only to the extent to which their performance does not endanger our self-preservation. Only the right of self-preservation is unconditional or absolute. The law of nature, which formulates man's natural duties, is not a law, properly speaking. Since the fundamental and absolute moral fact is a right and not a duty, the functions as well as the limits of civil society must be defined in terms of man's natural right and not in terms of his natural duty. The state has the function, not of producing or promoting a virtuous life, but of safeguarding the natural right of each. The power of the state finds its absolute limit in that natural right and in no other moral fact. If we may call liberalism that political doctrine which regards as the fundamental political fact the rights, as distinguished from the duties, of man and which identifies the function of the state with the protection or the safeguarding of those rights, we must say the founder of liberalism was Hobbes.[1]

An analogous characterization of Hobbes is given by

Michael Oakeshott, when in his profound commentary on *Leviathan* he observes that Hobbes expresses the morality of individuality and has in him more of the spirit of liberalism than many avowed liberals.[2] Finally, the Marxist interpretation of his thought, given by C. B. MacPherson, acknowledges Hobbes as the first and most distinguished spokesman for modern individualism.[3]

On the continent, we find another precursor of liberalism in Benedict de Spinoza (1632–1677), and one closer to the liberal tradition than was Hobbes. Spinoza shared many of Hobbes's assumptions about man and society: he ascribed to all human beings (as to every other thing in nature) an overriding inclination to self-preservation and insisted that human society be analyzed and understood in terms of the interactions of such necessarily self-serving agents. Like Hobbes, Spinoza sought to look anew at man and society, to understand social life in terms which did not confer on human beings a freedom denied to all other natural things, and, with Hobbes, Spinoza took power and natural rights as the two, mutually defining terms of his political theory. Both were unequivocal modernists rejecting as confusing or irrelevant to their common purpose the inherited vocabulary of moral and political notions of the dominant Aristotelian and Christian traditions. Despite all such similarities, the two thinkers diverge on crucial points. For Hobbes, peace is the necessary condition of all human goods, and the office of the government is solely to assure it. Liberty, which is the silence of the law, is only unimpeded action in pursuit of the individual's current desires, and is guaranteed in civil society only insofar as peace is not endangered. In Spinoza's thought, however, peace and freedom are conceived as conditions of one another. The social union is a condition whereby men develop their powers in freedom, and the office of government is as much to protect freedom as it is to keep the peace. In Spinoza, by contrast with Hobbes, the freedom of the individual is not a negative value, the absence of obstacles to the satisfaction of desires, but the supreme end of every individual. For human individuals aim to persist in being, according to Spinoza, not just to avoid death, but in order to assert themselves in the world as the individuals they are. Each human being, then, seeks to enjoy

the exercise of his own powers in freedom, for it is only so that
he can assert himself in his distinct individuality. The best
political organization to this end is not, as in Hobbes,
authoritarian government, but a democracy in which the liberal freedoms of thought, expression and association are
guaranteed. As much of an individualist as Hobbes, and as far
from the classical traditions of Western political philosophy,
Spinoza is closer to us and to liberalism in putting freedom at
the heart of his political thought. Stuart Hampshire expresses
this well when he says of Spinoza that he is on our side of the
barrier of modernity, and is to be contrasted with Aristotle:

> Slavery was not for Aristotle an evil, even less the principal
> evil. The notions of freedom and of liberation are not to be
> found at the center of Aristotle's ethics and philosophy of
> mind. There is no place here for the suggestion that sup-
> posedly free men are in a state of servitude, because of ignor-
> ance and thoughtless emotions, and that they had to be liber-
> ated through philosophical conversion, which will overturn
> many of their common sense beliefs. The exercise of the cru-
> cial powers of mind, of real intelligence and good feeling, is
> not represented as a liberation from a natural state in which
> these faculties are blocked and not available. Nature and free-
> dom are not in opposition. Similarly, his (Aristotle's) political
> thought does not have a place for freedom of individual choice
> as a value on the same level as justice in social arrangements;
> nor for respect for independence or a ground for action
> alongside respect for duties and obligations.[4]

Spinoza is closer to liberalism than Hobbes in seeing the
freedom of the individual as an intrinsic value – as, indeed, a
necessary ingredient in the best life, and a necessary condition
of any good life. For all this, Spinoza is not a liberal. Neither
he nor Hobbes endorsed the meliorist outlook of liberalism –
the belief that human affairs are subject to indefinite improvement into an open future. Doubtless each of them supposed
his reflections to be capable, if properly applied, of alleviating
the human lot, but for both of them the horizons of improvement were clouded by the permanent disabilities of human
existence. Whereas, for Hobbes, civil society was always
likely to fall back into a barbarous natural condition of war-
fare, for Spinoza the free man would always be a rarity; most

human individuals and most societies would always be ruled by passion and illusion rather than reason. For both of them, ignorance and slavery are man's natural condition, and enlightenment and freedom are exceptions in the life of the species. They are precursors of liberalism rather than liberals, because they did not share the liberal faith (or illusion) that freedom and reason can become the rule among men.

Hobbes and Spinoza belong then to the pre-history of liberalism, and we see in their case, as in others, that the emergence of the liberal movement as a clearly identifiable phenomenon encompasses a variety of complex influences. Towards the end of the medieval period, the Spanish Jesuits of the School of Salamanca had anticipated some of the themes of the classical liberals of the Scottish Enlightenment when they argued that, against certain background conditions, the just price of any commodity was the market price. For the most part, however, this contribution, like the contribution of various late medieval nominalists, was soon lost and had little influence on the liberal intellectual tradition, even if it figures as a context for many of the discussions in Locke's writings. The chief contribution of the medieval period was not a contribution in the realm of theory; it was rather a contribution through the inheritance of practical traditions of decentralized government and impartial law, eclipsed in continental Europe only with the rise of early modern absolutist monarchy. The dissolution of feudalism as a social system meant for the most part the loss of these traditions, but in England they were passed on to modernity through the Glorious Revolution and given a stronger individualist interpretation and application.

It is in the period of Whig ascendancy following the Glorious Revolution, in the debates during the English Civil War and, most importantly, in John Locke's *Second Treatise on Civil Government*,[5] that the central elements of the liberal outlook crystallized for the first time into a coherent intellectual tradition expressed in a powerful, if often divided and conflicted political movement. At the level of practice, English liberalism at this time comprehended a strong assertion of parliamentary government under the rule of law against monarchical absolutism, together with an emphasis on freedom of association and private property. It was these aspects of English political experience that Locke theorized and embodied in his conception of *civil society* – the society of free men, equal under the rule of law, bound together by no common purpose but sharing a respect for each others' rights. Nor was the civil society which Locke theorized a recent development within the English experience. As Alan Macfarlane has shown in his *Origins of English Individualism*,[6] English society was individualist in its legal traditions, its property laws and its family life and moral culture for several centuries before the Civil War. It was on the basis of several hundred years of social and economic development on an individualist model that Locke and other theorists of the Whig cause developed their conception of civil association under limited government.

Locke's thought harbors a number of themes which confer a distinctive complexion on English liberalism that persists up to the time of John Stuart Mill. It is, in the first place, firmly embedded in the context of Christian theism. As John Dunn has shown in his brilliant study,[7] Locke's doctrine of natural rights is fully intelligible only in the context of his conception of a natural law which is the expression of the divine nature. Natural rights in Locke embody the conditions we need in order to protect and preserve our lives under the natural laws given us by God. Under these laws, we have a right to liberty and the acquisition of property with which none may interfere, but, because we remain God's property, we may not alienate our liberty completely and irreversibly, as in a contract of slavery, and we are not permitted to alienate our lives by suicide. As God's creatures, we may acquire unencumbered rights over nature[8] and over objects we have ourselves manufactured, but we enjoy and exercise our liberty to do so under God-given laws. This complex of ideas, in which liberal ownership rights are legitimated within the context of Christian theism, remains characteristic of liberalism in England for three centuries after the publication of Locke's principal political writings.

Locke's thought brings to the fore a theme absent or denied in the thought of Hobbes and Spinoza – the theme of the links between the right to personal property and individual liberty.

There is in Locke what is lacking in earlier individualist writers – a clear perception that personal independence presupposes private property, securely protected under the rule of law. After Locke, the claim that a civil society demands the widespread diffusion of personal property becomes a staple theme of liberal writing, and it is this insight which embodies Locke's greatest contribution to liberalism. His theory of knowledge may be indefensible, and hardly consistent with his account of the foundation of natural law in divine ordinance, his detailed theory of property may be obscure and controversial[9] and be associated with a theory of value as conferred by human labor which was to be a source of weakness in later liberal theorizing. But his claim that liberty comes to naught in the absence of weighty rights to private property made a permanent mark on political thought and gives English liberalism one of its defining features.

By contrast with Hobbes and Spinoza, Locke is a liberal in virtue of the comparative optimism which pervades his thought. Unlike Hobbes, Locke imagined the state of nature to be a social condition, in which men are generally peaceful and good-willing and guide their conduct by their knowledge of the requirements of natural law. Men come to create a sovereign authority, not because they would prey upon one another without one, but because it is inconvenient that they should be judges in their own cases in the state of nature. The frailty that generates civil government in Locke is far less radical than that which drives men to it in Hobbes – it is simply a failing in impartiality. Further, in passing from the state of nature into the civil condition men lose only the liberty to punish themselves violations of their natural rights. Government does no more for them than protect the rights which they possessed before. Locke's view of natural man is, then, far less pessimistic than that of the pre-liberal individualists. If he did not subscribe to any doctrine of progress such as that propagated in the French Enlightenment, Locke nevertheless belongs with the liberals in seeing no inherent obstacle to the permanent establishment of a free society. He undoubtedly believed the struggles against absolute monarchy in his own society to be exemplifications of the movement against

arbitrary rule demanded by natural law, and civil society to be
achievable by all men.

The popular movement against monarchical absolutism in
seventeenth-century England had several peculiar ingre-
dients, some of which were to prove influential in the later
evolution of English liberalism. One of these was the myth of
the ancient constitution – of the laws and traditions of free
England before it had been subjected to the Norman Con-
quest – which was invoked by many of the more radical anti-
royalists and parliamentarians. Among the Levellers, Lilburn
refers to

> the greatest mischief of all, and the oppressing bondage of
> England ever since the Norman yoke, is a law called the com-
> mon law – Magna Charta itself, being but a beggarly thing,
> containing many marks of intolerable bondage, and the laws
> that have been made since by Parliament, have in very many
> particulars made our government much more oppressive and
> intolerable.

The legend of Anglo-Saxon freedom was to have a long life
among English reformers and radicals, so that when in 1780 it
was proposed that a Society for Constitutional Information be
established, the proposal stated that one of their objectives
was to conserve the records from which could be gleaned 'the
ancient usage and custom' of 'the venerable Constitution'
transmitted to us from our Anglo-Saxon ancestors. Again, as
W. H. Greenleaf has noted in his *Order, Empiricism and Politics,* when in 1806 J. Cartwright attacked the institution of a
standing army, he praised 'the sacred book of the Constitution, first composed in the Saxon tongue and the Saxon style'.
Finally, as Greenleaf notes in his recent masterly study, *The
British Political Tradition,* 'when in the crisis of 1848 *The
Economist* wrote 'Thank God we are Saxons' it was this array
of political ideas and virtues that was invoked; as similarly in
1855 when the doctrine of the ancient constitution was used in
its propaganda by the Administrative Reform Association.'[10]
The idea of an ancient constitution, then, continued to inspire
projects for radical reform on liberal lines well into the middle
decades of the nineteenth century.

A second important ingredient in seventeenth century
English liberalism was the foundational relationship in its

rhetoric and argument between doctrines of natural right and radical Protestant interpretations of scripture. Thomas Edwards, the Presbyterian constitutionalist, wrote that:

> All men are by nature the sons of Adam, and from him have derived a natural propriety, right and freedom. . . . By natural birth all men are equally and alike born to like propriety, liberty and freedom; and as we are delivered of God by the hand of nature into this world, every one with a natural innate freedom and propriety, even so we are to live, every one equally and alike, to enjoy his birthright and privilege.

Ruggiero asserted programatically that 'Jusnaturalism (natural law theory) is thus a kind of legal Protestantism'.[11] It is certainly clear that in England in the seventeenth century there was forged a link between political liberalism and religious dissent which was to endure right into the twentieth century. There is an important contrast here between the development of liberalism in England and that in France. In France, and in other Catholic countries such as Italy and Spain, liberalism always possessed a more pronounced free thinking and anticlerical bias than it ever acquired in England, and in those countries, also, religious dissent was not invariably associated with demands for religious toleration.[12] (The doctrines of the French Protestant thinker Calvin (1509–64) produced in Geneva one of the most repressive societies on record.) Again, in Germany the Protestant doctrines of Luther (1483–1546) had an authoritarian and not a liberal political implication. In Bohemia, it is true, the teachings of Jan Hus (1369–1415) affirmed the illegitimacy of appeals to papal and ecclesiastical authority in matters of conscience – a theme taken up by Hus partly under the influence of the English religious reformer John Wyclyf (1320–84). In general, it is fair to say that the demand for religious toleration was in most of Europe a by-product of the political struggle between Protestant and Catholic Churches, and only in England did the connection between religious nonconformism and liberal freedoms come to be firmly established over a period of several centuries.

3

Liberalism and the Enlightenment: The French, American and Scottish Contributions

Throughout the latter half of the eighteenth century, the history of liberalism in continental Europe and the spread of the Enlightenment must be regarded as aspects of one and the same current of thought and practice. This was not so in England, where the victory of the parliamentary forces in the Glorious Revolution of 1688 inaugurated a long period of social and political stability in an individualist order under the aegis of the Whig nobility. In France, liberalism emerged and developed against a background of feudal practices and absolutist institutions to which there is little analogy in English experience. For all the attempts of the Stuarts at installing a continental-style absolutist monarchy, longstanding English traditions inhibited the construction in England of anything like the social and political order of the French *ancien regime*. Further, as I have already observed, the political strength of the Catholic Church in France, as elsewhere in Europe, conferred from the start a distinctive complexion on French liberalism by associating it with free thought and anticlericalism rather than with religious nonconformity. Given its background in a pre-individualist social and political order, French liberalism had from the beginning a less congenial environment in which to develop than was the case in England, and this is reflected in the tendency of French liberals to invoke the English experience against their own less individualist past. Accordingly, the French liberal movement in its earlier phases was markedly Anglophile and much of its criticism of the arbitrary power of government under the *ancien regime* depended upon an interpretation (not always historically accurate) of English continental development. Thus in his masterpiece, *L'Esprit des Lois (The Spirit of the Laws)* (1748), Montesquieu drew on his imperfect understanding of the English constitution to represent it as containing a system of checks and balances and a separation of powers in virtue of which the freedom of the individual was assured.

Though he did not share many of its characteristic excesses, Charles Louis de Secondat, Baron de Montesquieu (1689–1755) is a representative figure of the French Enlightenment. In addition to describing and defending against all species of despotism and tyranny a form of constitutional government under the rule of law, Montesquieu in *L'Esprit des Lois* advocated and exemplified a naturalistic approach to the study of political and social life – one which emphasized the influence on social institutions and behavior of geographical, climatic and other natural conditions. Inconsistently and uncertainly, Montesquieu's work displays the commitment to a science of society shared by all the thinkers of the Enlightenment from Condorcet to David Hume. It is important, in this connection, to distinguish the movement we call the Enlightenment from an earlier, and in many ways deeper current of thought in France – that of the sceptical humanism of the *libertins erudits* of the early seventeenth century. These sceptics were the descendants of the new Pyrrhonists of the sixteenth century who had rediscovered the scepticism of the ancient Greek philosophers Pyrrho and his disciple Sextus Empiricus. Among the Pyrrhonists Michel de Montaigne and Pierre Charron are perhaps the most noteworthy, though the great sceptic Pierre Bayle should not go unmentioned as having through his monumental *Dictionaire historique et critique* (1740) contributed to the Enlightenment project of an encyclopedia of all knowledge. In spirit and temper, however,

the sceptical *libertins erudits* could not be further removed
from the *philosophes* of the Enlightenment. Like the latter,
the sixteenth- and seventeenth-century sceptics were opponents of superstition and fanaticism and exponents of toler-
ance in matters of belief and conscience; but, because of their
debts to the Greek Sophists and sceptics, and especially to
Sextus Empiricus, they had no hopes of a science of human
nature and society. Nor did they share the faith in progress
which animated many of the *philosophes*, but especially
Diderot (1713–84) and Condorcet (1743–94). Above all, their
sceptical distrust of the human reason led the Pyrrhonists to
humility rather than disbelief in regard to the mysteries and
dogmas of revealed religion: they recommended submission
to the Church in all outward matters, and left open the win-
dow to faith, provided its expression be free of all intolerance.

By contrast, the *philosophes* of the eighteenth century harbored extravagant hopes of human reason. These are most
memorably epitomized in Condorcet's *The History of Human
Progress* (1794). In that book, written (ironically enough)
when Condorcet was in hiding from the Revolutionary Terror, he sets out the meliorist doctrine of liberalism in its purest
and least compromising form – as a doctrine of human perfectibility. This is the claim that nothing in human nature or the
human circumstance prevents the achievement of a society in
which all the natural evils are suppressed and the immemorial
human follies – war, tyranny, intolerance – abolished. This
perfectibilist doctrine even rejects classical ideas of perfection
as overly static: rather, it asserts that human life is open to
improvement indefinitely, without ascertainable limit, into an
open future. This perfectibilist view is not only a conception
of human nature as lacking in any tragic flaw, but also a
philosophy of history. Among the Greeks and Romans, it
opines, learning and letters flourished, and ethics and politics
were subject to reasoned inquiry; but the arrival of Christianity thwarted the natural tendency to progress and initiated a
dark age of ignorance and slavery of mind and body. In
Condorcet, as in William Godwin, a near-contemporary of
Condorcet's who in his *Political Justice* (1798) argued for the
self-perfectibility of mankind through the exercise of reason,
the expectation of improvement is not a hope, but a faith; it is

grounded in the assertion of a law of progress, whose workings can be delayed or obstructed but never prevented. In these liberals of the Enlightenment, the liberal commitment to reform and improvement becomes a theodicy, part of a religion of humanity, and acquires the character of necessity. As Condorcet puts it, with unwitting irony:

> And how admirably calculated is this view of the human race, emancipated from its chains, released alike from the dominion of chance as well as from that of the enemies of its progress, and advancing with a firm and indeviate step in the paths of truth to console the philosopher lamenting the errors, the flagrant acts of injustice, the crimes with which the earth is still polluted? It is the contemplation of this prospect that rewards him for all his efforts to assist the progress of reason and establishment of liberty. He dares to regard these efforts as a part of the eternal chain of the destiny of mankind . . . .[1]

By no means all of the French *philosophes* accorded this apodictic character to the idea of progress. One of the greatest of them, Voltaire, was closer to Hume in his expectation that periods of advance and improvements would, in the natural course of things, be succeeded by ones of regression and barbarism, and in his *Candide* (1759) produced an unforgettable satire on the optimistic belief (theorized in the philosophy of Liebniz) that this is the best of all possible worlds. Again, the Scottish philosophers, though they shared the *philosophes'* project of a science of human nature and society, none of them endorsed the claim that indefinite improvement was possible, or progress inevitable. In France itself, the interpretation of history as evincing the operation of a law of progress was subjected to devastating criticism by the Enlightenment's most formidable opponent, J. J. Rousseau, who paradoxically held himself to a version of the thesis of man's perfectibility. It was most shaken, however, not by Rousseau's criticisms, but by the experience of the French Revolution, in which many of the ideas of the *philosophes,* and indeed of their critic Rousseau, seemed to have been subject to a decisive self-refutation.

Just as it led in England through Edmund Burke's writings to the development of a form of conservatism in which liberal values are preserved but liberal hopes chastened, so in France the French Revolution spawned a disillusionist literature of liberal self-criticism. On the constructive side, it generated the program of *guarantism* developed during the 1830s and 1840s by a group known as 'doctrinaires' who were much influenced by another liberal Anglophile, Benjamin Constant, and led by F. P. G. Guizot. Guarantism was as much a reaction of liberal thinkers to the experiences of the French Revolution of 1789 as it was a genuine attempt to distill the constitutional experience of England into a doctrine of civil and political liberty. Greeted with enthusiasm by liberal figures and movements in England such as Charles James Fox, by many in America and France itself, the French Revolution soon disappointed liberal hopes of democracy and sharpened liberal fears of popular sovereignty. In England, as I have noted, it induced Edmund Burke, a leading Whig who had defended the secessionist claims of the American colonists, to lay down the theoretical foundations of English conservatism in his *Reflections on the French Revolution* (1790). In France, the Terror led the leading liberal thinkers to reconsider the optimism and rationalism of the Enlightenment and, in particular, to repudiate the totalitarian theory of democracy as the vehicle of a general will that had been adumbrated in the writings of J. J. Rousseau.

The most profound critic of Rousseau's theory of democracy was, in fact, the theorist who inspired the guarantist movement, Bemjamin Constant. In his *Ancient and Modern Liberty* (1819), Constant develops with great force and clarity a crucial distinction between liberty as a guaranteed sphere of personal independence and liberty as the entitlement to take part in government. He claims, further, that modern liberty is the liberty of independence, whereas ancient liberty – the liberty that Constant sees Rousseau as trying to revive – is the liberty of participation in collective decision-making. What is this modern liberty, for Constant, and how does he contrast it in greater detail with ancient liberty? He states his distinction thus:

> Liberty is every man's right to be subject to the law alone, the right of not being arrested, tried, put to death or in any way molested, by the caprice of one or more individuals. It is every one's right to express his own opinion, to attend to his own art, to come and go, to associate with others. It is, lastly, every

one's right to influence the adminstration of the state either by nominating all or some of its officers, or by his advice, demands and petitions, which the authorities are in a greater or less degree obliged to take into account.

Let us compare this liberty with that of the ancients. That consisted in the collective but direct exercise of many privileges of sovereignty, deliberating upon the public welfare, upon war and peace, voting upon laws, pronouncing judgment, examining accounts and so forth; but while the ancients regarded this as constituting liberty, they held that all this was compatible with the subjection of the individual to the power of the community . . . . Among the ancients, the individual, a sovereign in public affairs, is a slave in all private relations. Among the moderns, on the contrary, the individual, independent in his private life, is even in the freest states a sovereign only in appearance. His sovereignty is restricted, and almost always suspended; and if now and again he exercises it, he does so only in order to renounce it.[2]

It has already been pointed out that, taken literally, Constant's sharp dichotomy is not historically defensible. Its principal significance is the role it plays in Constant's thought, and in the activities of the Guarantists whom he inspired, in illuminating the fact, centrally important for all classical liberals, that individual liberty and popular democracy are contingently but not necessarily related. The same reservations about popular democracy are expressed in a much broader theoretical context by Alexis de Tocqueville in his famous *Democracy in America* (1835). Tocqueville's concerns in that work differ from Constant's in that he is anxious less about the dangers of totalitarian democracy as realized in the revolutionary Terror than he is anxious about the threat to individualism posed by mass democratic governance. Tocqueville never disputes the inevitability of democracy, but (like J. S. Mill, who was much influenced by his work) he is concerned to avert the peril of majority tyranny which democracy carries with it. Together with Constant, Tocqueville gave to post-revolutionary French liberalism its distinctive flavor of intransigent individualism and passionate pessimism about the future of liberty. So far as France and most of Europe was concerned, the pessimism of the great French liberals was justified, since during the second half of the nineteenth century and thereafter

the liberal movement was displaced by the socialist movement as the chief expression of progressive political opinion.

In its general outlines, the classic American contribution to
the liberal tradition was little less influenced by Enlightenment conceptions than the French, though other elements of
a very different sort (including the influence of Scottish
philosophy) are also present. It has sometimes been contended that liberalism in the English-speaking world had different sources, followed a distinct course and even consti-
tuted a tradition divergent and separate from that which
emerged and prevailed in France. For the most part, this
claim that French- and English-speaking liberalism encompasses two opposed traditions is the claim that, whereas
English liberalism conceived itself as founding the claim to
liberty on an appeal to ancient rights and historical precedent,
French liberalism comprehends a fundamental appeal to
abstract principles of natural rights. In respect to the English
case, it has already been observed that the seventeenth-century fathers of liberalism appeal not only to the historical
myth of the ancient constitution, but also to ideas of natural
right based in the authority of scripture. The interpretation of
liberalism as encompassed by two divergent traditions finds
little more support in the American case, where the appeal to
natural rights was prominent from the first. As
D. G. Ritchie remarks: 'When Lafayette sent the key of the
destroyed Bastille by Thomas Paine to George Washington,
he was, in a picturesque symbol, confessing the debt of France
to America.'[3] Indeed, the Declaration of Independence of
1776 had sanctioned the rebellion of the American colonists
against the British government by making explicit reference
to 'the natural and unalienable rights' of which they had been
deprived. Further, the famous Virginia Constitution of 1776,
with its invocation of the 'indubitable, inalienable and indefensible right' of the people to reform, alter or abolish unjust
government, makes an appeal to abstract principle (rather
than to an historical precedent) which was to exercise an influence over the French revolutionaries themselves.

There seems little justification in the American example,
then, for an interpretation which represents English-speaking
liberalism as primarily a movement in defense of ancient

liberties and the French movement as being the party of abstract speculation. No doubt the millenial history of autocracy in France made an appeal to ancient liberty even less plausible there than it was in England, but this is not to say that liberal claims were not supported there (as they were by Montesquieu and others) by an historical and social analysis which forswore the appeal to natural rights. Both 'English' and 'French' liberal movements employed historical analysis side by side with appeal to abstract principle and natural right.

In the American case, to be sure, the constitutionalist rebels embraced a wide variety of outlooks. This variety is reflected in the *Federalist Papers,* which comprehend attitudes ranging from Jeffersonian radicalism through Madisonian moderation to the American Toryism of Hamilton. The American liberal contribution to classical liberalism is, for this reason, no less internally complex than are the French and the English. It remains a single, integral tradition, notwithstanding, because all the American liberal constitutionalists, like the English Whigs and the French guarantists, sought to establish 'a government of laws, not of men', in the words of the Bill of Rights preceding the Constitution of Massachusetts of 1780. It is this aspiration, more than any other, which confers on classical liberalism an identity and a character in virtue of which it transcends its internal diversity, and which informs all the writings of the *Federalist Papers*. It should be noted here that, whereas the American constitutionalists shared much with the French Enlightenment, they did not have in common with the *philosophes* an enmity to Christianity. The American Constitution, as it emerged from the struggles of the War of Independence, is an authentically Lockean statement in that the right to life, liberty and the pursuit of happiness which it proclaims is grounded in a natural law conceived to be ordained by God. More generally, the spirit of the *Federalist Papers* is very different from that of the French Enlightenment inasmuch as the Federalists's writings are imbued with a sense of human imperfection which animates all their constitutional proposals. In this stress on human imperfectibility, the American constitutionalists are at one with the thinkers of the Scottish Enlightenment, by whose writings (especially those of Adam Smith) they were much influenced.

It is in the writings of the social philosophers and political economists of the Scottish Enlightenment that we find the first comprehensive statement in systematic form of the principles and foundations of liberalism. Among the French, as among the Americans, liberal thought was bound up at every point with a response to a particular crisis of political order. It is not that the thought of the Scottish philosophers was not conditioned by the historical context in which they found themselves, but rather that they aimed, as perhaps the great French and American liberals did not consistently do, to ground their liberal principles in a comprehensive account of human social development and a theory of social and economic structure whose terms had the status of natural laws and not merely of historical generalizations. This Scottish aspiration to a science of society in which liberal ideals are given a foundation in a theory of human nature and social order is present even in the writings on political and economic questions of the great sceptic, David Hume. In Hume, by contrast with the thinkers of the French Enlightenment, the defense of a liberal order invokes the facts of man's imperfection. In the *Treatise in Human Nature,* Hume cites men's restricted benevolence and intellectual limitations and the unalterable scarcity of the means of satisfying human needs as causes of the emergence of the basic principles of justice. These latter are given in what Hume calls the 'three fundamental laws of nature' – the laws of the stability of possessions, of their transference by consent and of the performance of promises. In his essay on 'The Idea of a Perfect Commonwealth', Hume goes further and sketches in utopian spirit the main outlines of a form of political order in which these laws of nature are fully embodied and individual liberty guaranteed under the rule of law. It is in Hume, indeed, despite his reputation as a conservative theorist, that we find the most powerful defense of the liberal system of limited government.

In its most influential forms, however, the liberal system of principles was expounded and defended by Adam Smith in his *Inquiry into the Nature and Causes of the Wealth of Nations* (1776). Smith's analysis in that work has three important features which were to be inherited by his liberal posterity. There is, first, the idea that human society develops through a series of distinct stages, epochs or systems, culminating in the commercial or free enterprise system. This conception marks an increased degree of historical sophistication over the idea, common among post-Renaissance civic humanist writers who were in other respects an important influence on the Scottish Enlightenment, and present in the writings of Machiavelli, that human history may be understood as a series of simple cycles of rise and decline in civilizations. Second, Smith acknowledges, as do all the great classical liberals, that changes in economic system go hand in hand with changes in political structure, so that the system of commercial liberty finds its natural counterpart in a constitutional order in which civil and political liberties are guaranteed. Finally, Smith's system is an avowedly individualist one, in which social institutions are understood as results of the actions of human individuals but not as being the execution of human intention or design. The system which Smith expounds is, in other words, a version of methodological individualism, with the individual human agent being at the terminus of every social explanation. The Smithian system is individualist in the moral sense, also, since it issues in his conception of *the system of natural liberty* in which each and every person possesses the greatest liberty compatible with a like liberty for every other.

Smith's theorizing is distinguished from earlier liberal theorizing, and from the less formal reflections of most of his French and American fellow-liberals, by its systematic and comprehensive character. Entirely consistent with his methodological individualism, Smith perceives – as later liberals, such as J. S. Mill, did not – that the distinction between the economic and the political sides of social life can never be altogether free from artificiality or arbitrariness, since there is a constant reciprocal interaction between them and, more importantly, they obey the same explanatory principles and conform to the same regularities. In this systematic approach Smith's work parallels and follows that of the other great thinkers of the Scottish Enlightenment – Adam Ferguson, David Ricardo and others – and, through Smith's friend and disciple, Edmund Burke, Smith's approach had a direct impact on liberal thought in England until the insights of the Scottish school were swamped and lost through the rise of Benthamite Philosophic Radicalism.

The Liberal Era

Nineteenth-century Europe, and especially nineteenth-century England, may with good reason be regarded as exemplifying the historical paradigm of a liberal civilization, A. J. P. Taylor has memorably captured the individualist character of English life during the century before the outbreak of the First World War:

> Until August 1914 a sensible, law-abiding Englishman could pass through life and hardly notice the existence of the state, beyond the post office and the policeman. He could live where he liked and as he liked. He had no official number or identity card. He could travel abroad or leave his country forever without a passport or any sort of official permission. He could exchange his money for any other currency without restriction or limit. He could buy goods from any country in the world on the same terms as he bought goods at home. For that matter, a foreigner could spend his life in this country without permit and without informing the police. Unlike the countries on the European continent, the state did not require its citizens to perform military service. An Englishman could enlist, if he chose, in the regular army, the navy or the territorials. He could also ignore, if he chose, the demands of national defense. Substantial householders were occasionally called on for jury service. Otherwise, only those helped the state who wished to do so . . . . It left the adult citizen alone.[1]

Many other writers have seen in nineteenth-century England a golden age of liberal theory and practice. Such an interpretation is defensible and need not be misleading, so long as we understand the complexity of what occurred during this period and, more particularly, provided we understand how liberalism of the classical variant yielded during these times to a new, revisionary liberalism which in many ways compromised or suppressed altogether the chief insights of the classical liberal school of Tocqueville, Constant, the Scottish philosophers and the authors of the *Federalist Papers*.

In the area of political practice, nineteenth-century England experienced some notable victories for the liberal movement. The Catholic Emancipation Act of 1829, the Reform Act of 1832 and the repeal of the Corn Laws in 1846, together with a host of minor measures, represented evidences of the strength of liberal agitation and opinion in England during these decades. The anti-Corn Law League, in particular, brought together a coalition of liberal and radical groups in support of free trade under the leadership of Richard Cobden and John Bright, whose views encapsulated the pure spirit of classical liberalism in opposing military adventures at the same time that they favored retrenchment in public expenditure. Cobden and Bright were successful in their campaign for free trade, and their liberal preference for low taxation and low state expenditure was transmitted to W. E. Gladstone, who translated it into public policy during his tenure as Chancellor of the Exchequer and then Prime Minister. Throughout the first part of the nineteenth century, at least, and arguably right up to the First World War, political practice in England was dominated by liberal attitudes, taken for granted as presuppositions of political activity, often associated with religious dissent and nonconformity, but spreading right across the religious and political spectrum to encompass nearly the entire political class.

That nineteenth-century England was in large governed by the precepts of classical liberalism cannot then be denied. At the same time, it is easy to oversimplify the period. In the domain of political and legislative practice, it is questionable whether there was any period in which an uncompromising principle of *laissez faire* was respected. The first Factory Acts were passed in the early decades of the country and represented an acceptance of the principle of governmental intervention in economic life. It is true, of course, that none of the classical economists of the Scottish or English schools subscribed to a view of the state as having only night-watchman functions,[2] but the salient point is that the classical economists nevertheless aspired for an individualist

minimum of state activity. As G. J. Goschen put the matter
in 1883:

> Whether we look to the events of successive years, to the acts
> of successive parliaments, or to the publication of successive
> parliaments, or to the publication of successive books, we see
> narrower and narrower limits assigned to the principle of
> "laissez faire", while the sphere of Government control and
> interference is expanding in ever widening circles.[2]

The fact is that, from at least the 1850s onwards, there is a
piecemeal expansion of governmental intervention and activity into many areas of life. Further, the political consensus or
classical liberal precepts was at no time altogether unbroken,
and was subject to a powerful challenge in the person and
thought of Benjamin Disraeli, who repudiated liberalism
altogether in favor of a romantic Toryism woven from his personal mythology.[3] Certainly by the 1870s, those in England
who continued to hold to classical liberal principles were anx-
iously conscious that the current of historical development
was turning against them. From about 1840 to 1860, it is true,
there is in the writings of the *laissez faire* advocates of the
Manchester School and of *The Economist* (on which Herbert
Spencer worked briefly) a confidence that the political victories of the 1840s presage a period of expanding liberty,
economic and personal, against a background of international
peace, but it was not long before Spencer and others came to
feel that the cause of liberty was being lost in practice and a
new age of militancy imminent.

In the realm of ideas, on the other hand, classical liberal
ideas were on the retreat for most of the nineteenth century in
England. The first rupture of nineteenth-century English
liberalism with classical liberalism was probably brought
about by Jeremy Bentham (1748–1832), founder of
Utilitarianism, and by Bentham's disciple, James Mill (1772–
1836). In many respects, Bentham was and always remained
a classical liberal. He was a strong advocate of *laissez faire* in
economic policy and non-intervention in foreign affairs and in
his advocacy of legal reform he was usually on the side of individual liberty. At the same time Bentham's moral and political philosophy, Utilitarianism, in committing what Hayek
has called the constructivist fallacy – the belief that social

institutions can be the object of successful rational redesign – provided a warrant for much later illiberal interventionist policy. For, whereas in the Scottish school the Principle of Utility had been used mainly as an explanatory principle for understanding the spontaneous emergence of social institutions, and was employed evaluatively only to assess entire social systems, it was deployed by Bentham to assess specific measures of policy. As his project of a moral arithmetic or felicific calculus suggests, Bentham imagined that the impact of different policies on the public welfare could be given an exact quantitative statement, so that the principle of Utility rather than any established political maxim should serve as the practical guide for legislators. In Bentham's own work this approach bore fruit only in his proposal for the Panopticon or Model Prison, but it had a powerful influence across a much wider area in later decades. It informs the work of his disciple, James Mill, especially in his *On Government,* in which a narrowly rationalistic defense of democracy is undertaken, and it is perhaps not mistaken to suppose that it enters into the attitudes of Sidney and Beatrice Webb, who in the twentieth century were prepared to defend on constructivist Utilitarian grounds the social engineering policies of the Stalin regime in the USSR. Not all of the practical effects of Utilitarian philosophy on practical policy were anti-liberal – it inspired reforms in public health, the civil service and local government which any liberal could support – but Bentham's Utilitarianism, as it was transmitted into public life via the movement of the Philosophic Radicals, brought about the transformation of the Utilitarian outlook from the form in which it had appeared in the writings of Adam Smith into a form in which it had an inherent tendency to spawn policies of interventionist social engineering.

The political philosophy of James Mill's son, John Stuart Mill (1806–1873), is in some respects closer to that of classical liberalism than was his father's or Bentham's, and in some respects farther removed from it. It is closer inasmuch as in *On Liberty* (1859), at least, Mill's commitment to liberal individualism is much more prominent than his commitment to Utilitarian social reform. Further, the Utilitarian ethic Mill expounds in his *Utilitarianism* (1854) is very different from

Bentham's in that it recognizes qualitative distinctions among pleasures which are in turn to be accounted for by reference to the role the various pleasures have in the promotion of individuality. On the other hand, in his vastly influential *Principles of Political Economy* (1848), Mill makes a distinction between production and distribution in economic life, such that distributive arrangements are held to be altogether a matter of social choice, which suppresses the classical liberal insight into the character of economic life as comprising a whole system of relations among which productive and distributive activities are inextricably mixed. It is this erroneous distinction, rather than Mill's exceptions to the rule of *laissez faire* or his occasional flirtations with socialist schemes, which marks his principal departure from classical liberalism and which constitutes his real connection with later liberal and Fabian thinkers. In making this distinction, Mill effectively completed the rupture in the development of the liberal tradition begun by Bentham and James Mill and created a system of thought which legitimated the interventionist and statist tendencies which grew ever stronger throughout the latter half of the nineteenth century in England. Significant as an influence in leading Mill's own thought in an illiberal direction was French Positivism and, especially, the work of August Comte (1798–1857), whose historicist and élitist conceptions exercised a strong hold over Mill even if he also criticized the antiindividualist complexion of Comtism. In this respect, even if it occurred contrary to his own intentions, Mill may be said to have imparted into English thought the illiberalism of the French ideologues.

Mill's role as the watershed thinker in the development of liberalism is widely recognized. Dicey observes that

> changes or fluctuations in Mill's . . . convictions, bearing as they do in many points upon legislative opinion, are at once the sign, and were in England, to a great extent, the cause, of the transition from . . . individualism . . . to . . . collectivism. His teaching specially affected the men who were just entering public life towards 1870. It prepared them at any rate to accept, if not to welcome, the collection which from that time onwards has gained increasing strength.[4]

L. T. Hobhouse, himself one of the leading theorists of 'the new Liberalism' put the same point more tersely, but not inaccurately, when he said of Mill that 'in his single person he spans the interval between the old and the new Liberalism'.[5] In truth, whereas Mill never altogether abandoned the classical liberal commitment best expressed in *On Liberty*, his attitudes to trade unions, to nationalism and to socialist experimentation represent the decisive breach in the intellectual fabric of the liberal tradition.

Classical liberal theorizing continued in nineteenth-century England during and after John Stuart Mill's lifetime. Over a very long life, Herbert Spencer (1820–1903) defended a stringent version of liberal *laissez faire,* with his *Social Statics* and *Principles of Ethics* repaying reading even today. For reasons which are not entirely clear, Spencer has been the victim of many decades of unjust neglect, and his real achievements in social and political theory have gone unappreciated. As Greenleaf aptly remarks: '. . . during most of the present century there has been little appreciation of Spencer's ability and importance. It is not too much to say that since his death in 1903 he has been little read or discussed and invariably dismissed in disparaging words.'[6] Yet it is in Spencer that we find the most complete and systematic application of the classical liberal Principle of Equal Freedom to the various domains of law and legislation, and Spencer's *Principles of Ethics* remains of great and permanent interest for that reason. The principal weakness of Spencer's philosophy lies not in the consistency with which he applied his principles to the questions of the day (since his Cassandra-like warnings were all too well borne out by twentieth-century experience), but in the scientific and 'synthetic' philosophy of evolutionism which he constructed in order to give a foundation to his liberal outlook. It was inevitable that, once his evolutionary political ethic was subjected to devastating criticisms by such figures as T. H. Huxley and Henry Sidgwick,[7] it should lose its hold on the leading minds of the age. Where the influence of Spencer's evolutionism persisted – in the minds of the Webbs and G. B. Shaw for example – it was associated, not with Spencer's own liberal outlook, but with an endorsement of twentieth-century totalitarian movements as embodying the post-liberal phase of social evolution. This ironic

development of Spencerian evolutionism suggests the frivol-
ity and absurdity of attempting to ground political principles
in any scientific doctrine, but it does not detract from
Spencer's achievement in developing in a systematic form the
classical liberal outlook and transmitting it to posterity.

A host of lesser figures, such as Thomas Hodgkin in the
early part of the century and Auberon Herbert towards the
end, produced valuable work in the classical liberal individualist tradition. But, aside from Spencer, whose influence
in England steadily declined, and Lord Acton, whose public
authority never rivalled that of J. S. Mill, the classical liberal
tradition in the later nineteenth century contained no really
major thinkers. By the time of the 1880s and 1890s, and certainly at the turn of the century, even the imperfect classical
liberal outlook of Mill was being supplanted by revisionist liberal ideas often inspired by Hegelian philosophy. Particularly
prominent among the revisionary liberals were T. H. Green
and B. Bosanquet, who argued against the mainly negative
conception of freedom as non-interference held by most of
the classical liberals in favor of a notion of effective freedom,
or freedom as ability. This more positive view of freedom led
naturally in the writings of these Hegelian liberals to a defense
of enhanced governmental activity and authority and to support for measures limiting contractual liberty. In the early
decades of our own century, this revisionary liberalism was
given its most systematic statement in the writings of L. T.
Hobhouse, whose work, *Liberalism* (1911), attempts a synthesis of the philosophies of Mill and Green. It may be said that,
with Hobhouse, the new revisionist liberalism, in which ideals
of distributive justice and social harmony supplant the older
conceptions of a system of natural liberals, had come in England altogether to dominate progressive opinion where it was
not avowedly socialist.

In the political realm, the catastrophe of the First World
War shattered the liberal world that had prevailed for the
century between 1815 and 1914. Admittedly, anti-liberal
movements had emerged in the 1870s and 1880s in Germany
and the United States and had successfully imposed protectionist and interventionist measures on economic life, and
even in England the Liberal Party had under Asquith and

Lloyd George largely abandoned classical liberal positions on economic freedom and limited government. Again, as I have already observed, it is a mistake to suppose that there was ever a period of pure *laissez faire,* and anti-liberal elements began to enter into the liberal tradition itself from the mid-1840s in the work of John Stuart Mill. In this connection, it is important to note that the decline of classical liberalism cannot be explained simply by a response to the abandonment of important classical liberal ideas by John Stuart Mill and others. Such developments in intellectual life reflected, and were in part caused by, the changes in the political environment brought about the expansion of democratic institutions. In retrospect, it seems inevitable that the liberal order should have waned, once its basic constitution – a constitution that in England was preserved only in tradition and convention – came to be regarded as alterable by political competition within a popular democracy. It was the necessities of the competition for votes in the emerging democracies of the late nineteenth century, rather than changes in intellectual life, which contributed most to the ending of the liberal era.

Despite these necessary qualifications, it remains true that, for those who came afterwards, the century from the Napoleonic Wars to the outbreak of the Great War was a century of almost uninterrupted liberal progress and achievement. That century encompassed the largest and most continuous growth in wealth in human history against a background of stable prices and freedom from major wars; an unprecedented enhancement of popular living standards side by side with a colossal expansion in population; and a steady increase in popular literacy, numeracy and culture. Wars were fought and lost – in the Crimea, the Franco-Prussian War, the Russo-Japanese outbreak and the Boer War – but they did not disrupt the steady growth of wealth or undermine the system of freedom in the liberal policies of Europe. Depressions and recessions came and went, but the dominance of the international gold standard secured economic stability even through the worst economic dislocations of the 1870s. Even the tyrannies of this period are remarkable for their laxity and for the degree of individual liberty which they tolerated. Tsarist Russia, long regarded as the bastion of

pre-modern despotism in the historical mythology of the
European Enlightenment, was itself too badly organized to
achieve any significant degree of repression. Even under the
police-state system of the 1880s and 1890s during the reign of
Alexander III and the start of that of Nicholas II, when repression was at its worst and little was done to repress antisemi-
tic outrages, the Secret Police in Moscow consisted of six offi-
cials with a budget of £5000 for the entire province. As Norman Stone records,[8] by 1900 the security apparatus had barely
grown, there were almost no political prisoners and in the
huge province of Penza there were three police officers and 21
policemen.

   In Germany and elsewhere in Europe, it must be admitted,
developments were rarely favorable to the stability of a liberal
order of the sort that existed in England. In most countries,
liberalism and nationalism were fused in a synthesis which
was to play its part in the destruction of the international liberal order. In Germany the liberal movement was associated,
almost from the start, with nationalist ideals. Such ideals are
not prominent in the works of the greatest German liberal
thinkers – Immanuel Kant, W. von Humboldt and Friedrich
Schiller – but throughout the mid-nineteenth century,
liberalism's period of strongest influence in Germany,
nationalism was generally fused with the liberal movement.
In Kant's work, however, we find an extremely pure statement of the liberal ideal of limited government under the rule
of law – the ideal of individual freedom in a strictly rule-governed constitutional order which, under the name of
Rechtsstaat, is the counterpart in liberal German thought of
the Whig conception of civil association as theorized in England by Locke and of the French guarantist doctrine of Constant and Guizot. In Humboldt's early tract *On The Sphere
and Duties of Government* (1792), a defense of the rigorously
minimum state, more stringent than any found in Kant, is
given on the basis of Romantic ideals of individuality and self-
development: the state's activities are to be restricted entirely
to the prevention of coercion, he argues, because only in
that way can the widest expression of individuality be
secured. Humboldt's early work had an influence far beyond
Germany, most notably in England, where J. S. Mill used a

quotation from it as the epigraph to his *On Liberty* (1859). The political development of liberalism in Germany was brought to an end in the 1870s with the return to protectionism and the inception of welfarist policies by Bismarck. In Catholic Europe – France, Italy and Spain – the fortunes of liberalism remained linked with nationalism in its several forms and, despite occasional successes in specific areas of policy, liberal movements in these countries failed to establish any secure constitutional framework for the protection of liberty.

On the whole, however, Europe in the nineteenth century was and remained up until the Great War a liberal order: without passport control except in Turkey and Russia, it represented freedom of migration and the other basic liberties of an individualist system and, even where protectionist and welfarist policies supervened, the central elements of the rule of law were not abandoned. It was the First War which, almost overnight, brought to a head all the illiberal tendencies in thought and practice which had emerged in the latter decades of the century. A. J. P. Taylor has again captured brilliantly what the First War meant in the English experience:

> All this (the freedom of the English people) was changed by the impact of the Great War. The mass of the people became, for the first time, active citizens. Their lives were shaped by orders from above: they were required to serve the state instead of pursuing exclusively their own affairs. Five million men entered the armed forces, many of them (though a minority) under compulsion. The Englishman's food was limited, and its quality changed, by government order. His freedom of movement was restricted; his conditions of work prescribed. Some industries were reduced or closed, others artificially fostered. The publication of views was fettered. Street lights were dimmed, the sacred freedom of drinking was tampered with: licensed hours were cut down, and the beer watered by order. The very time on the clocks was changed. From 1916 onwards, every Englishman got up an hour earlier in Summer than he would otherwise have done, thanks to an act of Parliament. The state established a hold over its citizens which, though relaxed in peacetime, was never to be removed and which the Second World War was

again to increase. The history of the English people and of the English state merged for the first time.[9]

If there were signs of growing illiberalism in the last decades of the nineteenth century, the First World War broke the liberal order into pieces and initiated an era of wars and tyrannies. Nationalist movements, generally with few liberal elements, emerged everywhere from the collapse of the old empires, and in Germany and Russia totalitarian socialist regimes came to power which inflicted colossal injuries on their own populations and stifled liberty over most of the civilized world. In England between the wars J. M. Keynes, Beveridge and other revisionary liberals attempted to steer a middle way between the old capitalist order and the new socialist ideals, but intellectual opinion was largely dominated by Marxist doctrines which represented the liberal epoch as only a phase in a global development towards socialism. By the 1930s, indeed, there were few leaders of opinion who did not consider themselves critics or opponents of liberalism. The remnant of classical liberal thinkers who remained, such as Sir Ernest Benn[10] in England, wrote of the decline of liberty in elegiac vein. By the time the Second War broke out, it seemed that the liberal ideal had at last had its day, and the future would lie with more or less barbarous forms of statism.

The Revival of Classical Liberalism

The impact of the Second World War was to effect everywhere an enhancement of the scope and intensity of state activity. In Britain, the experience of a highly successful socialist command economy yielded the Beveridge Plan for a managed mixed economy, while in the United States war involvement entrenched the managerialist tendencies of the Roosevelt New Deal. In Europe, the political result of the war was to consign Eastern and Central Europe permanently to the sphere of influence of the Soviet totalitarian system and to bring to power socialist governments in much of the rest of Europe, including Britain. Where political opinion was not straightforwardly and explicitly socialist, there was a general consensus that the future lay with the activist state and the mixed and managed rather than the free market. The relative success of wartime planning convinced most opinion leaders that the same techniques could and should be used to promote full employment in a context of rapid economic growth and appeared to confer the authority of practical experience on J. M. Keynes's economic speculations. It seemed clear that classical liberalism, if it had been wounded by the catastrophe of the First War, had been killed off by the Second.

Even in the years of the Second World War and immediately thereafter, however, important contributions were made to intellectual life by thinkers whose allegiance lay with classical rather than modern or revisionist liberalism. Especially noteworthy here is F. A. Hayek's *The Road to Serfdom* (1944). Hayek's thesis was the bold and striking one that, contrary to all progressive opinion, argued that the roots of Nazism were in socialist thought and practice. Further, Hayek warned, the adoption of socialist policies by the Western nations would over the long run bring upon them the totalitarian nemesis. Any tolerable future for Western civilization would demand that socialist ideals be foresworn and the abandoned road of classical liberalism – the road to limited government under the rule of law – be travelled again. Whereas Hayek's thesis was ignored or derided in the English-speaking world, it was significant in Germany in adding strength to the current of neo-liberal thought which made possible that sudden abolition of economic controls which produced the postwar economic miracle. Hayek was crucially important, also, in initiating the formation of the Mont Pelerin Society, which kept classical liberal ideals alive throughout the postwar decades in which they were neglected or despised as anachronistic.

The postwar years produced other memorable statements of the liberal outlook. Karl Popper's *The Open Society and Its Enemies* (1945) argued that the Western intellectual tradition was in large part antipathetic to liberal civilization inasmuch as the dominant philosophical perspectives sponsored an authoritarian approach to the theory of knowledge. As against the philosophies of Plato, Aristotle, Hegel and the British empiricists, Popper urged a conception of human knowledge as having no foundation but as growing through the criticism and falsification of theories or conjectures. In political life, the path of reason was in the piecemeal reform of social institutions rather than the wholesale transformation of social life as envisaged by Marx and other Utopians. Popper's book had a wide influence outside professional philosophy, appealing to politicians such as Sir Edward Boyle in Britain and Helmut Schmidt in Germany as a statement of the epistemological as well as moral foundations of liberalism.

In the 1950s J. L. Talmon developed a powerful critique of various aspects of democratic theory in his *Origins of Totalitarian Democracy* (1952) and Sir Isaiah Berlin gave an exemplary statement of the liberal outlook in his *Two Concepts of Liberty* (1958). Berlin's lecture and subsequent book of that title were less significant, perhaps, in defending the negative idea of liberty as non-interference, than in grounding the worth of liberty on the conflict of values in human affairs. His thesis was that human experience testifies to an ineradicable and ultimate diversity of competing values for which no overarching standard of arbitration exists. The value of choice, and therefore of individual liberty, derives precisely from this radical pluralism of values.[1] As well as providing a timely restatement of the liberal outlook, Berlin's *Two Concepts of Liberty* made a permanent contribution to the liberal intellectual tradition in connecting the worth of liberty to the reality of moral conflict.

The quarter of a century after the end of the Second War is commonly characterized as the period of Keynesian consensus. Against the background of the destruction wrought by the War, over two decades of rapid economic growth ensued, most spectacularly in the nations whose defeat in the conflict – Germany and Japan – allowed for a radical overhaul of institutions and parties in the immediate postwar period. Dissident voices were hard to find during this period of apparently undisturbed prosperity. In 1960 F. A. Hayek, who more than any single figure is responsible for the revival of classical liberalism in the postwar period, published his masterpiece, *The Constitution of Liberty*. Without doubt the most profound and distinguished statement of the case of liberty this century, the book did not receive until the late 1970s the recognition it deserved[2] and its criticisms of revisionary liberal conceptions of social justice and welfarism fell on deaf ears.

Aside from his contributions to political philosophy, Hayek's work is significant in containing the most sophisticated reconstruction of the central ideas of the Austrian School of Economics which had dominated intellectual life at the London School of Economics when in the 1930s it was led by Hayek and Lionel Robbins. Drawing on the work of the founder of the Austrian School of Economics, Carl Menger (1840–1921), and on the ideas of his teacher, F. von Wieser (1851–1926), Hayek constructed a system of economic theory which conserved the central insights of the classical economists but corrected their most disabling fallacies. By contrast with the classical economists, Hayek's neo-Austrian system repudiates any objectivist theory of value. In Hayek's subjectivist view, economic value – the value of an asset or resource – is conferred on it by the preferences or valuations of individuals and not by any of its objective properties (such as its physical constitution or the amount of human labor needed to make it). Hayek's subjectivist methodology in economics led him to reject the ideas of general equilibrium found in neo-classical writers and to question the validity of macroeconomics (the study of entire economies or systems) as such. Macroeconomic theory – as found in Hayek's cóntemporary, J. M. Keynes – leads easily to the mistake of conferring on statistical fictions and aggregative judgments a causal role which they cannot possess in the real world. Hayek's microeconomic perspective, and the individualist and subjectivist methodology which supported it, went out of favor with the Second War and the long period of postwar expansion in which Keynes's ideas appeared to be vindicated.

Only with the disintegration of the Keynesian paradigm in the late 1970s did a wider public look again at the theories and insights of the Austrian school, but notable restatements of it were made in the United States by L. von Mises, Murray Rothbard and Israel Kirzner. The chief insight of the school that applied to the recessionary circumstance of the mid-1970s was that inflationary monetary policies, in changing the climate of expectations among decision-makers, were in the long run bound to be self-defeating. The stimulus to the economy produced by monetary expansion was effective only insofar as it was not generally expected. Once inflationary policy came to be taken for granted, it would necessarily fail to have the expansionary effect on the economy, and in particular on the level of employment, which was its goal. As against the Keynesian, and in opposition also to the monetary theorists of the Chicago School (such as Milton Friedman) who advocated monetary control as the means to stable growth, the Austrians maintained that the principal cause of the stagnation of the late 1970s was the discoordination of relative prices induced by governmental intervention. Rejected in the 1930s and ignored for 30 years after the Second War, this view has now come to be seen as increasingly compelling. Significantly, though the Austrian school deviates in fundamental respects from the theoretical presuppositions of classical economic thought, the policy implications of the Austrian analysis[3] of economic breakdown or depression in the 1930s or in the 1970s are essentially those of the classical economists in their heroic period – governmental withdrawal from the economy and the roll-back of restrictionist practices across the board.[4]

The early 1970s witnessed an extraordinary revival of liberal ideas in political philosophy. John Rawls in his *A Theory of Justice* (1971) developed a liberal conception of social organization which, despite its egalitarian orientation, had many links with classical liberal concerns for the priority of individual liberty within a rule-governed constitutional order. In his *Anarchy, State, and Utopia* (1974) Robert Nozick, incidentally criticizing Rawls's theory of justice, developed a most powerful defense of the stringently minimum state which had a massive impact on intellectual opinion in legitimating classical liberal ideas among professional philosophers. Nozick's work was of particular importance in reclaiming for the liberal tradition the utopian vision which virtually all liberals (with the exception of Hayek[5]) had rejected as uncongenial to the pluralism demanded by the liberal ideal. Instead of repudiating utopianism, Nozick proposed that the institutions of the minimal state be regarded as constituting the framework of the liberal meta-utopia – the political order within which individuals might in combination attempt to bring to practical realization their several and diverse utopian visions. Nozick's work was important, also, in emphasizing the connection between the defense of economic freedom and the worth of personal liberties of a non-economic sort – liberties of speech and lifestyle, for example. In this respect Nozick's restatement of classical liberalism contrasts sharply with the conservative defense of the free market which has long been a tradition on the American Right.

By the mid-1970s the resurgence of classical economic theory had been accorded public recognition by the award to Hayek and Friedman of the Nobel Prize. A few years later, their ideas and proposals were common currency, cited by such figures as Margaret Thatcher and Ronald Reagan and widely perceived – by the enemies as well as the friends of liberalism – as having acquired a real political importance. Whether the association of classical liberal ideas and rhetoric with the free-market conservatism of the late 1970s and early 1980s will contribute to the long-run strength of the classical liberal revival is, of course, a disputable point. The conjunction of free market conservatism with illiberal policies in the areas of personal and civil liberties,[6] and the likely failure of the inconsistent and partial attempts at restoring free markets to deliver the growth demanded by the democratic public, suggest that the political strength of classical liberalism may prove to be short lived.

The intellectual presence of classical liberalism is unlikely to be so evanescent. Its concerns are those of the age – the overexpansion of government, with all the dangers to liberty that it entails, and the control of policy by rivalrous special interests whose machinations defeat the public interest – and in many areas of thought it has produced scholarship of the first order. In the writings of Hayek, the work of the Public Choice School, and especially in the writings of James Buchanan,[7] we find an inquiry into the conditions of constitutional government fully as profound as any produced by the eighteenth-century political economists. In Buchanan's foundational contribution to the Public Choice School, the methodological perspective of Austrian economic theory is extended to the activities of states, bureaucracies and politicians, and the phenomenon of government failure – the inability of governments to deliver public goods – is convincingly explained. In its normative or prescriptive dimensions, Buchanan's work is vitally significant in developing an argument for a new constitutional contract which has yet to be addressed even by most classical liberals. Only by revising fundamental constitutional rules, Buchanan argues, can the domination of government by special interests be prevented and the classical functions of the liberal state effectively performed. Like Hayek's, Buchanan's work shares the concerns, and achieves the intellectual distinction, of the great classical political economists.

PART TWO:
PHILOSOPHICAL

6

The Search for
Foundations

Ever since its emergence as a definite strand of thought and
practice in early modern Europe, liberalism has been pre-
occupied with an inquiry into its own foundations. As a movement set to challenge many of the traditions of the societies in
which it came to birth, liberalism could not rest content with
a self-image in which it was only an episode in the adventure
of modernity. All the great liberal theorists sought a foundation for their commitment to individual liberty which was not
merely local in its scope, but potentially universal. Liberal
demands were seen by liberals themselves as the demands,
not of any sectional interest or cultural circle, but of all
humanity. The justification of liberalism, for this reason, must
be compelling for all men, and not only for the few who live
already in individualist societies. How did liberal thinkers go
about finding a foundation for the liberal commitment?

   Though many liberal writers appeal to more than one set of
arguments to support their principles of equal liberty and
limited government under the rule of law, it is useful to distinguish three separate strands of justification for liberal principles within the liberal intellectual tradition. The first of these
is the doctrine of natural rights, classically expounded by John
Locke and invoked in our own time by Robert Nozick.
According to this theory, it is a fundamental moral truth
that human beings may make valid and weighty claims in
justice against each other, society and government. Human
beings possess the moral rights in virtue of which they may
make these claims of justice, not as members of any specific

moral community or as subjects of any positive legal order, but simply in virtue of their nature as the sort of creatures they are. The natural rights ascribed to human beings in this theory are natural, accordingly, in the sense that they are pre-conventional, morally prior to any social institution or contractual arrangement, and they are natural in the related sense, also, of being grounded in the natures of the creatures that possess them. In Locke explicitly, and implicitly in all natural rights theorists, claims about natural rights presuppose deeper claims about natural law. By natural law is meant here the theory that there are certain moral necessities, certain principles of just conduct, which flow directly from an independently identifiable human good. The matrix of any theory of natural rights, then, is an account of natural law. In the absence of an account of natural law, indeed, natural rights theories are not wholly coherent or finally defensible: the rights they yield are otherwise stillborn, deprived of the environment in which alone they can be conceived and brought to birth.

The difficulties involved in constructing a plausible theory of natural rights today are formidable and in all likelihood insuperable. They are, in part, difficulties to do with explicating natural law in a modern framework of ideas which excludes anything like a natural teleology. Whereas in Locke natural law is sustained by divine will, from which it derives its moral content, Aristotle supports his moral theory with a metaphysical biology which depends in the last resort on a mystical conception of nature as a system tending to perfection. There seems little room for Aristotelian and Lockean ideas of final causes or natural ends in a modern scientific worldview which has expelled teleology from itself, where it has not given the evidences of purpose in nature a mechanistic explanation. As Spinoza saw, we are left with things and men in all their miscellaneous diversity and particularity, once the metaphysic of final causes is abandoned and with it the idea of nature as comprising a teleological system. This is to say, in short, that the conception of natural law needed to support a theory of natural rights is incompatible with modern empiricism. It may be, as I shall suggest later, that an attenuated or tempered version of natural law doctrine may be given an empiricist translation, but the content of such a slimmed-down theory will be exclusionary rather than positive, setting limits to what is a viable morality rather than selecting any specific morality. This conclusion is accepted in a backhanded fashion by Alasdair MacIntyre, when after noting that 'any adequate teleological account must provide us with some clear and defensible account of the *telos*; and any adequate generally Aristotelian account must supply a teleological account which can replace Aristotle's metaphysical biology', goes on to concede everything to modern scepticism with the assertion that 'the good life for man is the life spent in seeking the good life for men'.[1]

There are other, no less damaging objections to any enterprise of grounding a specific morality, personal or political, on the demands of human nature. According to contemporary theorists of natural rights,[2] such rights embody the conditions necessary for the flourishing of man as the distinctive creature he is: we discern the content of these rights by considering the distinguishing marks of the human species and the circumstances in which these characteristics or powers might best be realized. First of all, however, as Bernard Williams observes:

> a palpable degree of evaluation has already gone into the selection of the distinguishing mark which is given this role, such as rationality or creativity. If one approached without preconceptions the question of finding characteristics which differentiate men from other animals, one could as well, on these principles, end up with a morality which exhorted men to spend as much time as possible in making fire; or developing peculiarly human physical characteristics; or having sexual intercourse without regard to season; or despoiling the environment and upsetting the balance of nature; or killing things for fun.

Aside from the arbitrariness of the moral judgments which go into any selection of the distinguishing mark of man, there is also (as Williams goes on to observe) the moral ambiguity of many distinctive human characteristics. Imagination and sensitivity may be expressed in sophisticated cruelty, as courage may be in evil causes. As Williams justly concludes: 'If we offer as the supreme moral imperative that old cry, "be a man!'', it is terrible to think of many of the ways in which it could be taken literally.[2]

These difficulties in natural law doctrine may, perhaps, be illustrated by a thought-experiment. Let us suppose we are in a position (one we may well occupy in the middle future, given the possibilities of genetic engineering) to alter the content of man's nature or essence: how could the natural law ethic of realizing man's distinctive powers help us here? We might refuse to alter human nature, and be wise to do so; but the reason can hardly be that human nature as it is embodies moral perfection. If it does not – and few would dare claim that it does – then we must choose which human powers to foster and which to repress or remold. No ethic which appeals solely to an idea of realizing the distinctive human powers can help us with the radical choice as to, 'Which essence shall man have?' Yet this thought-experiment is only a dramatic metaphor for the sorts of decisions men must sometimes take as individuals and societies. The sort of conflict that is experienced when such radical choices are made has its source in the fact that the virtues in which the distinctive human powers are expressed are often incompatible and uncombinable: one excellence crowds out another, life is short, and a choice of a form of life often involves a deliberate amputation of one part of a man's nature. As Stuart Hampshire has argued:[3]

> It is notorious that Aristotle gives no convincing reason why there must be, as a matter of conceptual necessity, something that is identifiable *a priori* as the best form of life for a man. Aristotle argued that there must be such a discoverable norm, because otherwise our desires would be empty and vain, and our reasoning in support of judgments of the goodness of this or that would never be conclusive. The norm is easily discoverable *a priori*: the standard and normal form of life must be one that is the perfect development of human potentialities, rather as the life cycle of a species of plant is the realization of the essential potentialities of that species. We only need to inspect the concept of the human soul in order to draw the bare outline of the kind of life, the system of activities, which constitute the norm for an intelligent living being; the moral philosopher's secondary skill is to fill in this bare outline with concrete illustration and detail. If the best and standard form of life is the full expression of the potentialities specific to

human beings, as it must be, in Aristotle's philosophy, it follows that it must be the form of life that a good man wants. For
a good man is simply a man who conspicuously possesses, and
manifests in action, the potentialities that, taken together, distinguish human beings from other creatures. Thus the circle is
conveniently completed.

But the circle has some notoriously dubious arcs. We cannot suppose that there must be some one form of life, called
"the good for man," identifiable *a priori*, merely because it is
a condition of conclusiveness in practical reasoning that there
should be such a norm. Nor can we argue that our desires and
interests are empty and unintelligible, if wanting, or being
interested in, something cannot always be shown to be, at one
or two removes, a case of wanting, or being interested, in
some single all-inclusive and final thing. That ends of action
should be stated in a conjunctive form, and should permit conflicts that cannot always be settled by one overriding criterion,
which is sufficiently definite to count as a criterion, is not in
itself an unintelligible suggestion. To admit an irreducible
plurality of ends is to admit a limit to practical reasoning, and
to admit that some substantial decisions are not to be
explained, and not to be justified as the right decisions, by any
rational calculation. This is a possibility that cannot be con-
ceptually excluded, even if it makes satisfying theoretical
reconstruction of the different uses of "good," as a target-set-
ting term, impossible.

This last consideration – that the various components of
human flourishing may often be in intractable conflict with
one another – seems to me to be decisive against any prospect
of reviving a natural law ethics.

I have not here touched upon questions as to how natural
rights theories deal with circumstances of moral catastrophe
or practical emergency, nor have I addressed the possibility of
conflicts within the system of natural rights. It is, in general,
a problem for all natural rights theories whether they specify
only one basic natural right – to liberty, to property or whatever – and, if so, how they account for other important moral
claims. Alternatively, if a plurality of natural rights be
allowed, there is a question as to whether these rights may
come into conflict with each other and, if so, how such conflicts may be resolved. No satisfactory treatment of these
questions is to be found in Locke's writings, and they have

continued to trouble liberal theorists in our own time. Recent attempts to specify a set of compossible or nonconflictable rights[4] succeed only at the formal level: they fail to give those rights an adequate content. Once the reality be acknowledged of conflict within the system of rights, or of the system of rights as a whole with other considerations, it seems hard to avoid the sort of pluralistic balancing of claims which the natural law ethic aims to preclude. And once it be accepted that the elements of human well being are complex and on occasion conflict, so that promoting choice-making, say, may compete with the provision of peace or security, this kind of moral conflict cannot be ruled out.

None of this suggests that something akin to the minimum content of natural law, as theorized in the writings of H. L. A. Hart and Stuart Hampshire,[5] may not be defensible. It is at least plausible to regard some moral constraints as partly constitutive of any viable human community – though the concept of viability at stake here is necessarily open-textured and only partly determinate. It is some such conception of the natural necessities of human social life that David Hume invokes when he grounds his laws of human nature on the contingent but unalterable facts of scarcity and the limitation of human benevolence. This more empirical statement in minimalist form of a natural law approach will surely exclude some societies and moralities – those of Marxist communism or National Socialism – but it will not uniquely select liberal morality or society. There is, for this reason, no direct route from a theory of human nature to the superiority of a liberal society.

An alternative approach to the justification of liberal rights is found in the philosophy of Kant which seeks to avoid altogether any appeal to human nature or well being. In part, Kant argues that a conception of human beings as bearers of weighty rights to freedom and justice is presupposed by our conceptions of them as being always ends in themselves and never only means to the ends of others. This is a transcendental argument which reasons from features of our standard moral thought and practice back to the principles or presuppositions in virtue of which that moral life is possible. In addition, Kant appears to have supposed that only a principle conferring the maximum equal freedom on human beings – the classical principle of liberalism – would satisfy the demand of universalizability imposed by the categorical imperative. A liberal society was, in effect, the only social order acceptable to persons who conceived themselves to be autonomous rational agents and ends in themselves. It may well be doubted that Kant's arguments succeed in justifying liberal principles. Insofar as they are, indeed, purely formal and appeal only to the presuppositions of practical reasoning, it is reasonable to suppose that they will achieve far less in the way of grounding substantive principles than Kant (or subsequent Kantians) hoped. To the extent that Kant's argument draws surreptitiously on anthropological assumptions, he deviates from his own method of justification in ethics. Even if such deviations be allowed in a spirit of charity, it is far from clear that Kant's program succeeds. The conception of ourselves as autonomous rational agents and authors of our own values bears patently upon it the marks of modernity and European individuality and has no universality as an image of moral life. In Kant's own case, the idea of autonomy trades heavily on a metaphysical conception of the noumenal self which is clearly recognizable as the emaciated shadow of the immortal soul of Christian traditions. Once Kant's metaphysic of the self is abandoned, there is nothing in his argument which favors liberal principles as uniquely appropriate for human beings.

The moral force of natural rights theories at the time of their inception in the seventeenth century was to resist doctrines of monarchical absolutism and patriarchal rule. In the twentieth century, their force is primarily to combat moral relativism on the one hand and utilitarianism on the other. Many contemporary liberal rights theorists are concerned to mark a sharp distinction between the deontic considerations specified by claims of right and the aggregative or teleological considerations specified by arguments from welfare on the other. Such a sharp distinction was alien to the liberal tradition in Continental Europe until Kant's work became influential, and it became prominent in British liberal thought only after Bentham had turned utilitarian moral appraisal into a closed system of ideas. In the Scottish school utilitarian arguments about general welfare are used to support claims about

justice and no necessary incompatibility is admitted between deontic and teleological moral claims. The attempt
to ground moral rights on a utilitarian theory is, in effect,
resumed by John Stuart Mill in *On Liberty,* and is there generally judged to be unsuccessful. The traditional argument
against Mill is that, unless it is assumed that the protection of
liberty and the promotion of general welfare are never competing ends – and such an assumption appears to be plausible
only in a theistic context of the sort accepted by Locke and
Adam Smith – then the supreme principle of utility will sometimes sanction restraints of liberty which classical liberals
(and many others) cannot but regard as unjust. Against this,
it has been argued that the Principle of Utility appropriately
applies only to whole social systems and not to specific acts or
rules and that, if an indirect utilitarianism of this sort be
adopted, it will favor the the liberal system of greatest equal
liberty over all others.

   This is the argument I developed myself in my book, *Mill
on Liberty: A Defence.*[6] It turns on three moves. First, there
is the claim that in Mill the Principle of Utility is axiological
and not practical in force – it is a principle for the evaluation
of whole codes of rules or social systems and not one that is to
be invoked directly by legislators or private individuals to
settle questions of conduct. If, as this indirect utilitarian
approach maintains, the Principle of Utility imposes no moral
obligation on anyone to maximize welfare, then assenting to
it as the ultimate principle of evaluation may be compatible
with endorsing non-utilitarian maxims in practical life. Sec-
ondly, there is the claim that direct utilitarian policy is self-
defeating, so that we are in effect bound to adopt non-utilitarian maxims in practical life. The third and most crucial move
is from indirect utilitarianism to liberalism – from the general
argument against welfare – maximization as a policy entailed
by the Principle of Utility to a specific argument that it is the
Principle of Liberty that is so entailed. Mill's specific argument to this last claim is in large part psychological: it is an
appeal to the character of individuality as a necessary ingredient of human happiness. For Mill, happiness is a condition
of successful activity in which individuals express their distinctive natures. It is as one of the dimensions of autonomy, and

thereby one of the conditions of individuality, that liberty is thus important as a condition of happiness.

Mill's argument has several real virtues. It succeeds in showing the place of activity and choice-making in human happiness and thereby in forging a necessary link between happiness and freedom which in the utilitarian ethics of Bentham and James Mill was neglected or only fortuitous. By enriching the classical utilitarian conception of happiness with Aristotelian and Humboldtian elements, Mill softened the tension between the moral individualism of the liberal outlook and the collectivist implications of the classical utilitarian goal of general welfare. Further, Mill's indirect utilitarian reasoning demonstrated that, as any rate in a large range of circumstances, the adoption of non-utilitarian moral and political precepts could be defended on utilitarian grounds. These features of Mill's achievement in *On Liberty* bring his liberal outlook closer to the classical liberalism of the Scottish school. If Mill is successful in showing the importance of individuality as a necessary ingredient in human well being, he fails nonetheless in developing anything like a satisfactory account of liberal justice in utilitarian terms. In part this is because of the unsatisfactoriness of the Principle of Liberty he seeks to defend. This Principle – that individual liberty may not be restricted except to prevent harm to others – cannot fulfil the liberal role Mill wants for it, because of the intractably controversial character of the concept of harm which it incorporates and because, even if the concept of harm it contains could be adequately specified, the Principle would remain an insufficient guide to action. Let us look at these radical failings in Mill's enterprise.

The first difficulty is that of the indeterminacy of Mill's conception of harm. Nowhere in Mill's writings do we detect any awareness that, as it is employed in ordinary thought and practice, the concept of harm embodies substantive moral judgments and so cannot be neutral between rival moral outlooks. For the Principle of Liberty to be able to arbitrate cases of moral conflict, the controversial value-judgments embodied in ordinary uses of the notion of harm would need to be screened out and a conception of harm having the characteristic of moral neutrality successfully defended. This is a task Mill never attempts. Even if it could be achieved, Mill's Principle of Liberty would still be unsatisfactory. It states only a *necessary* condition of justified liberty-limitation and can never tell us when restricting liberty is on balance justified without the help of Mill's sovereign Principle of Utility. That this is so is unavoidable, given Mill's utilitarian commitment and the form in which his Principle of Liberty is stated, but it disables the latter as a principle of liberal justice. The protection afforded to individual liberty by Mill's Principle will be absolute only in the self-regarding area where actions do not harm the interests of others. Whenever there is harm or a risk of harm to others, liberty restriction is in principle justified – and may always be justified on balance if the calculus of utilities shows that such restriction promotes the general welfare. Further, and crucially, nothing in Mill's Principle requires that the resultant distribution of freedom and unfreedom be equitable. In many cases, harm may be prevented, and the general welfare promoted, by liberty-restricting policies that impose grossly unequal and inequitable burdens on different social groups. In order to avoid this result, Mill's Principle would need further supplementation by a Principle of Equity or Fairness – a Principle, in other words, that is in competition with the utilitarian concern for general welfare. Though Mill may succeed in deriving the Principle of Liberty from that of Utility, it seems clear that a Principle of Equity regulating the distribution of freedom would sometimes conflict with the promotion of general welfare. Such a Principle guaranteeing equity in the distribution of freedom seems indispensable to any genuinely liberal theory of justice and to be indefensible in utilitarian terms. Insofar, then, as Mill's project was the project of reconciling the utilitarian concern with general welfare with liberal concerns about the priority and equal distribution of liberty, it was a project foredoomed to failure, since it must remain thoroughly implausible that a utilitarian policy of harm-prevention would always respect constraints of equity on the consequent distribution of unfreedom.

These failings in the Millian project are, in part, a central motivation in the recent revival of contractarian approaches in the justification of liberal principles. In its most powerful

and plausible form in the work of John Rawls,[7] the contractarian approach sheds the vestigial moral collectivism of Mill's
utilitarianism and abandons concern with promotion of the
general welfare. Rawls's contractarian approach is authentically individualist in a way Mill's utilitarian ethics cannot be,
since it confers on individuals in the original position a veto
against policies which would maximize general welfare while
invading the liberty and damaging the interests of some. (I set
aside in this discussion the difficulties – which I believe to be
insoluble – involved in anyone acquiring a knowledge of the
utilitarian effects of different distributional policies that is
detailed enough to guide action.) Rawls's theory of justice as
fairness has several other decisive advantages over Mill's
approach. The Principle of Liberty yielded by the contractarian method is not a harm principle such as Mill's, with all its
ambiguities and dangers, but instead the classical liberal
Greatest Equal Liberty Principle, which imposes a constraint
of justice on all welfarist policy. It is for this reason that
Rawls's theory is closer to classical liberalism than Mill's: for,
though the maximin principle gives priority to the worst off in
society in condemning as unjust any inequalities which do not
benefit them, the first principle of Rawls's theory – the
Greatest Equal Liberty Principle – prohibits the unjust dis-
tributions of unfreedom allowed by Mill's Principle. Again, it
is to be noted that the redistribution demanded by the Difference Principle is the only function accorded to government
apart from the protection of liberty, perfectionist and utilitarian policies for the promotion of art, science or the general
welfare being excluded as inconsistent with the demands of
justice. The contractarian method as practised in Rawls's
work, because of its underlying individualism in ethical
theory, has an inherent advantage over any utilitarian theory
as a defense of liberal freedoms.

None of this is intended to suggest that Rawlsian contractarian theory is without serious difficulties. It is unclear to me
that the redistributional Difference Principle can be given a
contractarian derivation, or that the Greatest Equal Liberty
Principle can be (as Rawls supposes) neutral in respect of the
economic system, capitalist or socialist, to which it applies.
Neither of these difficulties compromises the achievement of

Rawls's theory in developing an individualist defense of the liberal order in contractarian terms. Rawls's work links up with that of James Buchanan in the Public Choice School[8] in seeking to ground liberal freedoms on minimal moral postulates and an individualist conception of value. It foreswears both the spurious claim to rational universality of natural rights and the aggregative pretensions of utilitarian ethics and asks instead what constitutional principles would prove acceptable to individuals ignorant of their own specific conceptions of the good life. The contractarian approach, as exemplified in different ways in the work of Rawls and Buchanan, accepts the moral diversity of modernity as an ultimate fact and seeks to construct principles of justice which permit rival moral traditions to coexist in peace. The conception of the human individual deployed in contractarian theory may vary greatly – from a conception of Kantian inspiration in Rawls to one of Hobbesian derivation in Buchanan and the kindred work of David Gauthier[9] – but common to all contractarian approaches is the enterprise of grounding common constitutional principles on an uncompromising individualist ethical foundation. It is in the development of this contractarian method that the most promising solution of liberalism's foundational questions is to be found.

The Idea of Freedom

Is there a conception of liberty that is distinctively liberal? It is often argued that the conception of freedom employed by classical liberal writers is wholly or predominantly a negative one, whereas revisionary liberals and socialists invoke a more positive conception. This contention is not altogether mistaken, but it can prove misleading so long as the complexity of the distinction between positive and negative liberty is not firmly grasped. In its simplest and clearest form, the distinction is that marked by Constant, and stated in our own time with unsurpassed insight by Isaiah Berlin,[1] between non-interference and independence on the one hand and an entitlement to participate in collective decision-making on the other hand. In this sense, certainly, all the classical liberals were exponents of a negative conception of liberty. Neither Locke, Kant, Smith, or even John Stuart Mill ever doubted that individual liberty could be suppressed in a society where every adult has an entitlement to a voice in government. At the same time, the negative conception of liberty is not restricted in its uses to liberals, since both Bentham and Hobbes – the former a quasi-liberal at best, and the latter an individualist and authoritarian and never a liberal – employ it in a particularly clear and uncompromising form. There seems to be no necessary connection between holding to a negative view of liberty and espousing liberal principles, even if advocacy of the positive view has often gone with opposition to liberalism.

What, then, is the positive view of freedom? In its uses in Hegel and his followers, it is the view that individual freedom in the full sense involves having an opportunity for self-realization (or, perhaps, even presupposes the achievement of self-realization). The political content of the positive view is that, if certain resources, powers or abilities are needed for self-realization to be effectively achievable, then having these resources must be considered part of freedom itself. It is on this basis that modern revisionary liberals have defended the welfare state as a freedom-enhancing institution: it is alleged to confer needed resources on individuals and thereby to expand their chances of freedom. These revisionary liberals need not be disciples of Hegel, but they share with him the view that liberty (positive liberty) involves more than having the legal right to act. It signifies, primarily and centrally, having the resources and opportunities to act so as to make the best of one's life. Often enough, such revisionary liberals also assume that positive or genuine liberty can be achieved only in a harmonious or integrated society.

This Hegelian conception of positive liberty has been powerfully criticized by Berlin and other contemporary liberals. They point out, first, that liberty and self-realization are not one thing, but two: a man may freely choose to sacrifice his chances of self-realization for the sake of a goal he values more highly. Further, it is far from clear in any given case what self-realization involves. Who is to say what self-realization entails for any man? It may be that, just as one man's requirements for self-realization often conflict with those of other men, so the requirements for self-realization may be conflicting or competitive even in a single man. Finally, modern classical liberals reject the Hegelian version of positive freedom because, as F. A. Hayek has pointed out,[2] it results in the end in the equation of liberty with the power to act – an equation inimical to the liberal ideal of equal freedom because power cannot by its nature be distributed equally. There seems to be an insuperable conflict between the Hegelian conception of positive freedom and liberal values of diversity and equality.

Not every conception of positive freedom is so demonstrably opposed to liberal values as the Hegelian view. It is worth recalling that both Spinoza and Kant deployed a positive view of freedom as autonomy or individual self-determination in defense of toleration and limited government. This is a view not of freedom as collective self-determination, but rather as the rational self-government of the individual agent. It informs Mill's most liberal work, *On Liberty*, and it has roots in liberalism's pre-history in the Stoic writers. This version of the positive view seems entirely congenial to liberal concerns and to have an assured place within the liberal intellectual tradition. This individualist variant of the positive idea of freedom illuminates another dimension of the distinction between negative and positive freedom. This is the difference between conceptions of freedom which make of it always and only an interpersonal relationship and those (the positive conceptions) which allow that individual freedom may be curbed by internal constraints as well as by social obstacles. In its most persuasive form, this positive view is the view of freedom as the non-restriction of options – whether by other men's obstruction or by factors internal to the agent himself, such as weakness of will, irrational fantasies or inhibitions or uncriticized socialization to conventional norms. The idea of freedom as non-restriction of options[3] is connected with the idea of the autonomous individual – the individual who is not ruled by others, and who rules himself. This idea of the autonomous individual is central in Kant's philosophy as well as Spinoza's and must rank as one of the key notions of the liberal tradition.

Freedom as autonomy has been much criticized by contemporary liberals. For Berlin,[4] it involves the mistaken bifurcation of the self into two parts, the higher and the lower, the rational and the desirous, the essential and the empirical, and is easily used as a license for paternalism and tyranny. For Hayek,[5] the idea of autonomy (as it figures in John Stuart Mill, for example) involves representing as threats to individual freedom what are, in part, its conditions – obedience to conventional norms and subscriptions to inherited forms of life. Berlin's criticism certainly applies to some variants of the positive view, but it is not clear that it need apply to all. Conceptions of autonomy may themselves be relatively open or closed insofar as they imply that autonomous agents are bound to converge on a single form of life or agree on a unified body of truths. Though most or all of the classical conceptions of freedom as autonomy – in the Stoics, Spinoza and in Kant – are in this sense closed conceptions, it may be possible to construct an account of autonomy which does not have the feature of requiring access to a single body of objective moral truths, but instead demands simply the free exercise of the human intelligence. Many modern threats to freedom – propaganda, media manipulation and the tyranny of fashion – can be understood, I think, only by invoking some such conception of autonomy. Freedom may be curbed by means other than coercion, and it is a virtue of the idea of freedom as autonomy (in contrast with the more stringently negative view) that it accommodates this fact. Again, Hayek is on strong ground in detecting in Mill a hostility to convention as in itself inimical to freedom that must in the end be illiberal. No free society can long survive (as Mill himself recognized in other moods[6]) without stable moral traditions and social conventions: the alternative to such norms is not individuality, but coercion and anomie. A conception of autonomy that is plausible and defensible need not be infused with the animus towards convention and traditions that pervades some of Mill's writings. The ideal of autonomy, as it figures in social psychology, connotes not the inner-directed man who is unmindful of his social environment, but rather the critical and self-critical man whose allegiance to his society's norms is informed by the best exercise of his rational powers. Such an open conception of autonomy, which avoids the rationalist metaphysic of the self of the sort criticized by Berlin and which has an insight into the role of conventions and traditions as conditions of freedom that was denied to Mill, seems entirely congenial to liberalism.

How does such a conception of freedom as autonomy bear upon the specific liberties to which we often refer as the liberal freedoms? I mean here such freedoms as those of speech and expression, association and movement, occupation and lifestyle, and so on – the freedoms which Rawls has perceptively termed 'basic liberties'.[7] Rawls himself was motivated to develop his account of the basic liberties by the indeterminacy of the idea of the greatest liberty: the demand that liberty be maximised (and equalized) is given a definite content, he notes, only when liberty is decomposed or disaggregated into a set or system of basic liberties. I suggest that the basic liberties be conceived as framing the necessary conditions of autonomous agency. A free man is one who possesses the rights and privileges needed for him to think and act autonomously – to rule himself, and not be ruled by another.[8] The content of the system of basic liberties need not be fixed or immutable, but will embody the conditions necessary in a given historical circumstance for the growth and exercise of powers of autonomous thought and action. It is clear that, whatever else they may include, the basic liberties will encompass the juridical protections of a liberal state – freedom from arbitrary arrest, of conscience, association, movement and so forth. In addition to these civil freedoms, it has often been contended that the basic liberties include economic freedoms, variously conceived. Indeed, one of the demarcation criteria for modern as opposed to classical liberalism is the suggestion (made by modern or revisionary liberals) that freedom as autonomy presupposes governmental provision of economic resources and governmental correction of the market process. As against these modern liberals, and in opposition to Rawls who constructs the set of basic liberties so as to be neutral in regard to operations of economic organization, I shall in the next chapter submit that classical liberals are right in their assertion that individual freedom presupposes the juridical protection of contractual liberty and weighty rights to private property.

8

Individual Liberty, Private Property and the Market Economy

According to all the classical liberal thinkers, a commitment to individual liberty implies endorsement of the institutions of private property and the free market. Against this classical liberal view, Marxists and other socialists have argued that private property is itself a constraint upon liberty, and revisionary liberals of the modern school have argued that property rights must sometimes be overridden by the demands of other rights, including rights to positive freedoms of various sorts. My aim in this chapter is to suggest that these socialist and revisionary liberal claims neglect the vital role, theorized in the classical liberal intellectual tradition, that the institution of private property and its corollary, the free market, play in constituting and protecting the basic liberties of the individual. In addition to defending the institution of private property as at once a condition and a component of individual liberty, I will submit that free markets represent the only non-coercive means of coordinating economic activity in a complex industrial society. By contrast with revisionist liberalism, my contention is that private property is the embodiment of individual liberty in its most primordial form and market freedoms are indivisible components of the basic liberties of the person.

We may begin our inquiry by recalling the link, long noted by classical liberals, between having a property in one's

person and being a free man. For anyone to have a property
in his person means, in the first place and at the least, that he
has disposition over his talents, abilities and labor. Unless this
requirement of self-ownership be satisfied, human beings are
chattels – the property of another (as in the institution of slavery) or a resource of the community (as in a socialist state).
This is because, if I lack the right to control my own body and
labor, I cannot act to achieve my own goals and realize my
own values: I must submit my ends to those of another, or to
the requirements of a collective decision-procedure. Having
this most basic property right in my own person seems to
entail having many of the standard liberal freedoms – contractual liberty, liberty of occupation, association and movement
and so on – and it is compromised whenever these freedoms
are abridged. The connection between property and the
basic liberties is in these cases constitutive and not just
instrumental.

Having a property in oneself is, for these reasons, one element in being a free man or an autonomous agent. I do not say
that having or exercising that property right is all there is to
individual liberty, or that all property rights can be justified so
directly as elements of liberty. Recognizing the constitutive
role of property in the person in the liberty of the individual
does not, by itself, tell us anything about the justification or
character of property rights in natural resources or the means
of production. Robert Nozick has perceptively noted the
difficulties of Locke's theory of the initial acquisition of property rights by mixing one's labor in them.[1] It can fairly be said
that no adequate theory of initial acquisition exists, and in
particular that no determinate process of initial acquisition
has been shown to flow from the primordial property right
each man has in his person. There are nevertheless powerful
considerations – of Humean rather than Lockean inspiration
– that go far to show that the property right each of us has in
his person cannot be effectively exercised in the absence of
the opportunities afforded by the system of private or several
property. This is to say that the system of full liberal ownership – which is Honore's term[2] for unencumbered and exclu-
sive rights of control and disposition – can be defended
by arguments about the necessary conditions of effective

self-ownership which do not depend upon a Lockean account of acquisition.

The central argument linking private property with self-ownership appeals to the character of private property as an institutional vehicle for decentralized decision-making. In any society, men will have different and conflicting goals and values, which will make competing demands on resources. Further, each man always has his own stock of knowledge, often tacit or practical knowledge unavailable to him in theoretical or explicit terms, on which he draws in action – knowledge of his own preferences and their ranking and structure, but also of his own specific circumstances and environment. Decentralizing decision-making to the level of the individual, as in a system of full liberal ownership, permits individuals to act on their own values and use their own knowledge subject to minimal constraint from other individuals. How is this? The question may be approached at once from the standpoint of the individual's knowledge and that of his values or goals. As to his knowledge, we must recognize that the practical character of much of our knowledge itself creates a presumption in favor of private property. By practical knowledge I mean here the knowledge discussed by such philosophers as Oakeshott, Polanyi and Ryle[3] – knowledge stored or embodied in habits, dispositions, skills and traditions. This is knowledge available principally in use, and it is difficult or impossible to collect it and transfer it in usable form to any collective body. Such knowledge may indeed be embedded in the practices of a corporate body – a medieval monastery, an Oxford college or a family firm – and it is unavoidably present in some measure even in large bureaucratic organizations, where it sustains otherwise unworkable structures. The point is not that practical knowledge cannot exist save within private property institutions (since all institutions cannot help depending upon it), but rather that it is inevitably depleted and wasted in institutions which devolve decisions away from individuals, who are the carriers or bearers of tacit knowledge, to collective decision-procedures. In other words, as we move away from private property to communal or collective institutions, the practical knowledge available to society is diluted or attenuated. Nor is this only or mainly a matter of the size of the decision-making institution. Though tacit knowledge is certainly more likely to be generated and used well in a small communal institution – a kibbutz, say – than in any large planning institution, its use will always be limited by the fact that the possessors of practical knowledge will need to make it accessible to the other participants in the institution if it is to be the basis of common policies. As the history of attempts to foster entrepreneurship in socialist systems suggests, it is no easy task for the practical knowledge embodied in entrepreneurial perceptions to be transmitted to even a small collective body.

This last point is a perfectly general one, whose ramifications extend to the individual's values or goals. Here the vital insight is that, though in a system of full liberal ownership the individual is unavoidably constrained by the limitations of his own talents and resources, he is not constrained by the values or opinions which prevail among his neighbors. Subject only to the law of the land, he may use his property for any purpose he chooses: he need consult, or seek permission from, no one. Thus he may use his resources for ventures that would be judged excessively risky, or in violation of conventional moral, opinion by his neighbors. As Hayek has said:

> action by collective agreement is limited to instances where previous efforts have already created a common view, where opinion about what is desirable has become settled, and where the problem is that of choosing between possibilities already generally recognized, not that of discovering new possibilities.[4]

Communal systems of ownership, then, embody a bias against risk and novelty – a fact which may go far to explain the technological stagnation of the world's socialist economies. From the point of view of my argument, however, the dampening effect of communal institutions upon innovation is less fundamental than the pervasive restraint of liberty they involve. For, by contrast with private property institutions, communal ownership demands that, if the individual's projects are ever to be realized in practice, they must be acceptable to the dominant opinion of his society or, at least, of the other members of his cooperative. The defense of private property, then, is one that connects it with the autonomy of the individual – his ability effectively to implement his life-plans – and not just with negative liberty. One may even say that, whereas the constitutional framework of a liberal order protects the basic liberties in their formal or negative form, it is private property that embodies them in their material or positive form.

I have argued that private property is a guarantee of individual autonomy: but what of those who have none? It is an overly familiar objection to the institution of private property that, though it enhances the freedom of action of those with substantial resources, it does nothing for those who are not propertied. It may easily be conceded that the individual whose resources are wholly dependent on a wage or salary is, on my account, less autonomous (though not less negatively free) than one with substantial property. In recognition of this fact, all classical liberals have favored taxation policies which encourage the formation and wide diffusion of wealth and have resisted policies (such as those of inflationary government financing) which redistribute resources from income-earning groups to those with real assets.[5] It must also be noted, however, that, if one without property of his own is less autonomous in a free society than is the man of property, he remains more autonomous than he would be in a society whose productive assets are collectively owned. As Hayek has put it:

> That the freedom of the employed depends upon the existence of a great number and variety of employers is clear when we consider the situation that would exist if there were only one employer – namely, the state – and if taking employment were the only permitted means of livelihood . . . a consistent application of socialist principles, however much it might be disguised by the delegation of the power of employment to nominally independent public corporations and the like, would necessarily lead to the presence of a single employer. Whether this employer acted directly or indirectly he would clearly possess unlimited power to coerce the individual.[6]

The same point has been put trenchantly be Michael Oakeshott:

> We have, perhaps, been less successful, from the point of view of freedom, in our institution of property than in some of our

other arrangements, but there is no doubt about the general character of the institution of property most friendly to freedom: it will be one which allows the widest distribution and which discourages most effectively great and dangerous concentrations of this power. Nor is there any doubt about what this entails. It entails a right of private property – that is, an institution of property which allows to every adult member of the society an equal right to enjoy the ownership of his personal capacities and of anything else obtained by the methods of acquisition recognized in the society. This right, like every other right, is self-limiting: for example, it proscribes slavery, not arbitrarily, but because the right to own another man could never be a right enjoyed equally by every member of society . . . . The institution of property most favorable to liberty is, unquestionably, a right to private property least qualified by arbitrary limits and exclusions, for it is by this means only that the maximum diffusion of the power that springs from ownership may be achieved . . . . That a man is not free unless he enjoys a proprietary right over his own personal capacities and his labor is believed by everyone who uses freedom in the English sense. The freedom which separates a man from slavery is nothing but a freedom to choose and to move among autonomous, independent organizations, firms, purchasers of labor, and this implies private property in resources other than personal capacity. Whenever a means of production falls under the control of a single power, slavery in some measure follows.[7]

Finally, as one of the architects of the Soviet totalitarian state observed prophetically: 'In a country where the sole employer is the state, opposition means death by slow starvation. The old principle, who does not work shall not eat, has been replaced by a new one: who does not obey shall not eat.[8] The insight conveyed by these statements is that, though it is true that private property enhances the autonomy of its possessors, still the freedom that is generated by private property is not only that enjoyed or exercised by its holders. Those without substantial property in a private property society enjoy a degree of autonomy denied to any in a communal system in which no important decision can be taken without general agreement. Indeed, even the worst off in a private property system is more autonomous than most in a collective system: the vagabond is freer than the conscript soldier, even if (dubiously enough, in real-world socialist systems) the latter is better fed.

The defense I have sketched of private property in terms of its contribution to individual autonomy has a Humean beginning in competition for scarce resources, but it issues in a Kantian recognition that private property ensures personal independence. The two strands in the argument are distinct but not altogether unconnected. The Kantian strand insists that the individual must be conceived as author of his ends and goals, which he cannot be required to submit to the authority of any collective process beyond the rule of law, while the Humean argument invokes the scarcity of knowledge and of natural resources as permanent consideration in favor of private property. Taken together, these two strands of argument yield a powerful case for private property institutions. To be sure, they do not show that individuals living in a liberal state are in any way obliged to hold their property in the form of full liberal ownership: they may, if they so choose, vest their property in corporate bodies – cooperatives, monasteries, or whatever – and, in any real society, a host of such complex arrangements will be made. The basic juridical form of property right supported by the arguments I have advanced remains nonetheless full liberal ownership. It is worth recalling, at the same time, that (as Robert Nozick has noted[9]) a society based on such property rights need not be a capitalist or market-based society in its economic aspects: there is always the possibility that individuals might choose to conduct economic life on communalist or socialist principles, as they are fully entitled to do in the liberal order. The possibility is remote in any modern society, however, that large numbers of people will opt out of market relations in favor of communal arrangements. There are, in addition, strong positive reasons, akin to those which support the institution of private property, why the market process is likely to be dominant in the economic life of a liberal society.

By way of exploring the liberty-preserving role of the market, let us first recall a distinction made by Hayek[10] between the economy and the catallaxy. An economy, properly understood, is an allocation of resources within an organization, whether that be a family, a business corporation, a church or an army. The allocation of resources within an organization poses the problem, traditionally and wrongly conceived to be the central problem of economic theory, of utilizing scarce resources with maximum cost-efficiency. It presupposes that the purposes or goals of the organization and of its members may be ranked in a hierarchy of importance by reference to which the distribution of resources may then be determined. In the catallaxy – the economic life of many organizations in a whole society – there is no agreed hierarchy of ends and there is no authoritative allocator of resources. (The socialist project may be defined as that of turning the catallaxy into an economy proper – that is to say, into a purposeful organization.) The central problem of the catallaxy, as of economic theory properly understood, is *the division of knowledge in society* – the problem of how the knowledge that is dispersed or diffused among millions of economic agents, and known in its totality to no one, can be rendered accessible to many. This is the true role of the market process: not economizing on scarce means to known ends, but rather generating through the price mechanism information as to how economic agents ignorant of each other may best attain their equally unknown purposes. The task of the market is, then, that of a discovery procedure for identifying and transmitting to others data about the infinitely complex structure of preferences and resources in society.

Conceived in this way, the competitive market has several features which render it uniquely congenial to a liberal individualist society. The coordination it effects among human activities is, firstly and above all, non-coercive. Each agent adjusts his plans to the plans of others by reacting to the information about others' preferences and resources that is transmitted to him through price signals. The outcome of these adjustments is the tendency to coordination or equilibrium which is a feature of unhampered market activity. This is not, of course, the barely coherent general equilibrium of neoclassical economics, but instead the loose integration of purposes and activities which is observable in the real world market process. It is a form of coordination which is finer than any achievable by central planning, and one which at no point abrogates the liberty of individuals. Coercive techniques for the coordination of economic activity – the techniques of the Soviet system, for example – have been shown, both in theory and by historical experience, to be disastrously inferior in their results to those attained in even the hampered market economies of the West. This, after all, was the theoretical conclusion of the famous 'calculation debate'[11] of the 1920s and 1930s, in which the Austrian economists Mises and Hayek demonstrated conclusively the impossibility of rational resource-allocation in a socialist order. This theoretical result has been overwhelmingly corroborated by the historical experience of central economic planning, which is an experience of shortage, malinvestment, black markets and dependency on Western capital, technology and foodstuffs. As well as being non-coercive, then, and partly in virtue of that very reason, the market process is more efficient than planning or coordination in producing harmony among men's economic activities. It is in this sense that the market may be considered the paradigm of *a spontaneous social order* and to illustrate Proudhon's dictum 'Liberty is the mother of order'.

It is a conventional objection to the view of the market process as a self-regulating system that I have sketched that market economies may be subject to breakdown or crisis. The Great Depression of the 1930s is often cited in this connection, as illustrating in acute form the cyclical disturbance to which market processes are liable. As an historical interpretation of the events leading up to the crash and economic collapse of 1929 and thereafter, the claim that it originated in endogeneous market disturbances is at once controversial and implausible. Economic historians inspired by very different traditions of economic thought[12] have argued convincingly that the causes of the Great Depression are to be found in large part in misconceived governmental intervention in the economy. This is not to deny that specific markets may on occasion exhibit disorder, volatility and speculative disturbance, nor even (as G. L. S. Shackle has noted[13]) to resist the claim that changes in tastes and expectations may conceivably produce large-scale episodes of economic maladjustment. It may well be, again, that economic life over the long wave displays a long-term cycle such as that theorized in the speculations of Kondratiev and other writers. That technological innovation and cultural change disrupt established patterns of economic activity, with entrepreneurship creating what Schumpeter[14] calls a wave of creative destruction across the economy, are facts too obvious to be denied in any theory. They show that a general equilibrium is not to be expected in any economic system (as might in any case have been inferred from the contradictory assumptions that are built into the very idea of a general equilibrium) but they cannot undermine the observed reality of a tendency to coordination in the market process. Even where episodes of market disorder are evident, we have no warrant to invoke such instances of market failure as conclusive grounds for government intervention. Every governmental intervention has real costs, and there is strong evidence that the vagaries of governmental policy constitute the chief source of economic disturbance in recent decades. It is a general truth, remarked by many of the classical economists, that the imperfections of the market are never sufficient to justify intervention in the absence of a careful consideration of the corollary reality of government failure. The historical experience of recent decades – in which a prolonged period of economic growth apparently stimulated by Keynesian policies of macro-economic management and deficit financing has been succeeded by one of deep stagflation – suggests not only that interventionist policies are self-limiting in their effects, but that they aggravate the disorders they are intended to cure. At the very least, there is no rational warrant for the conventional opinion that economic planning can do better than the free market.

The case for market freedoms has been set out in part in terms of efficiency and the clear failures of planning to deliver the promised goods, but the fundamental argument is one that invokes individual freedom itself. It is wholly unclear if notions of efficiency have any definite content aside from that which emerges from the voluntary transaction of the free market – though we are on firm ground in attributing inefficiency to any system in which free exchanges are thwarted, information costs escalated and the pattern of investment distorted. Even if a criterion of economic efficiency were available that is independent of the outcomes of the market process, and the market was found on occasion to fall short of this criterion, nothing suggests that government could do better. And, if it did, it could do so only by overriding the choices of individuals for the sake of a value of maximum efficiency whose claim on reason there is no warrant for accepting.

The Liberal State

What is implied by liberal principles for the constitutional or juridical form of the state? In the first place, it is clear that liberal principles enjoin the limitation of government by stringent rules. Liberal government cannot be other than limited government, since all strands within the liberal tradition confer upon persons rights or claims in justice which government must acknowledge and respect and which, indeed, may be invoked against government. The liberal state need not for this reason be a minimum state. Classical liberals such as Humboldt, Spencer and Nozick have argued, it is true, that the functions of the state must of necessity be restricted to the protection of rights and the upholding of justice, but this position has no clear warrant in liberal principles and is a minority view within the liberal tradition. The idea of a minimum state which does no more than protect rights is in any case an indeterminate idea until the rights that are to be protected have been given an adequate specification. Unless this specification has itself a liberal content, the minimum state could be a socialist state – if, for example, the basic rights were welfare rights, or positive rights to a share in the means of production. Again, as I shall later show in detail, the idea of a minimum state that protects only negative rights (against force and fraud) contains a radical incoherence in that it contains no plausible proposal for the financing of these minimum functions. There is, for this and other reasons, a fundamental difficulty in the account given by advocates of strong negative rights of the justification of the authority of the state. Advocacy of the minimum state is, in any case, not to be found in most liberal writers. Most liberals, and all the great classical liberals, acknowledge that the liberal state may have a range of service functions, going beyond rights-protection and the upholding of justice, and for this reason are not advocates of the minimum state but rather of limited government.

What, though, is the form of liberal limited government? It is clear that it need not be democratic government. Where it is unlimited, democratic government cannot be liberal government since it respects no domain of independence or liberty as being immune to invasion by governmental authority. Unlimited democratic government, from a liberal point of view, is rather a form of totalitarianism – the form predicted and criticized by J. S. Mill in *On Liberty*. No system of government in which property rights and basic liberties are open to revision by temporary political majorities can be regarded as satisfying liberal requirements. For this reason, an authoritarian type of government may sometimes do better from a liberal standpoint than a democratic regime, always provided that the governmental authorities are restricted in their activities by the rule of law. This observation yields the important insight about liberal government – an insight grasped by such classical liberals as the French guarantist theorists and the German exponents of the *Rechtsstaat* – that it is constitutional government. A liberal political order may take the form of a constitutional monarchy, as in Britain, or a constitutional republic, as in the United States, but it must contain constitutional constraints on the arbitrary exercise of governmental authority. Whether these constraints include bicameralism, the separation of powers between legislature, judiciary and executive, federalism and a written constitution, or some other mixture of devices, is less important than the fact that, in the absence of some such constitutional constraints on government, we cannot speak of the existence of a liberal order.

The institution of liberal limited government is for these reasons compatible with many varieties of democratic system (and with the restriction or absence of political democracy) and it may adopt a range of constitutional devices for the embodiment or protection of liberal principles and practices. It may rest the judicial protection of liberty on parliamentary government and constitutional convention, as in Britain, or it may seek to constrain both lawmakers and the judiciary by a written constitution. In its legal dimensions, the liberal state may rely primarily on the common law as interpreted by an independent judiciary, or else it may repose greater confidence in the legislative protection of liberty. The *sine qua non* of the liberal state in all its varieties is that governmental power and authority be limited by a system of constitutional rules and practices in which individual liberty and the equality of persons under the rule of law are respected.

In its classical phase, liberalism was often associated with the maxim of *laissez faire* and sometimes, though not commonly, with advocacy of the minimum state. Even John Stuart Mill was in his *Principle of Political Economy* (1848) prepared to treat *laissez faire* as the obvious general rule of public policy with each departure from it having to be argued for and justified against the background of a strong presumption in favor of non-interference. Again, Adam Smith and the other Scottish classical liberals allowed a range of governmental activities in social and economic life – in Smith's case, support for public schooling and the provision of public utilities of various sorts – which were hardly justifiable under a strict construction of *laissez faire*. These classical liberals allowed government important service functions, then, as has already been observed, yet they saw no conflict between such a position and their strong advocacy of economic freedom. How is this apparent contradiction to be understood and overcome?

We may begin to clarify this problem by noting an indeterminacy and an ambiguity in the slogan of *laissez faire* itself. Every advocate of *laissez faire* relies on a theory of justice or rights to tell him what is to count as an interference or an invasion of liberty. Judgments about violation of *laissez faire*, then, presuppose a theory of just entitlements to property and liberty, and these judgments will vary according to divergencies in the underlying theories. Thus some advocates of *laissez faire* will treat patent and bankruptcy laws as themselves constituting interferences with economic liberty, whereas others will treat them as framing the just framework for economic activity. Such differences can be resolved only by reference to a theory of just holdings which gives the slogan of *laissez faire* a definite content, and I have argued in earlier chapters that no satisfactory account exists of natural rights which might supply such a theory. (I shall sketch later what I take to be a

more adequate account of liberal justice, conceived in contractarian terms.) Aside from this basic indeterminacy, the
idea of *laissez faire* also contains a more specific ambiguity.
The early classical liberals were concerned, primarily and
almost exclusively, with coercive or proscriptive governmental involvement in the economy. They attacked tariffs and
regulations which imposed legal constraints on economic
activity, and for the most part they were content if such constraints were removed. They did not, in other words, demand
a complete withdrawal of government from economic life.
This is not an inconsistent position (even if it may be criticiza-
ble in other ways) once it is understood that government
activity may take coercive or non-coercive forms. John Stuart
Mill theorized this distinction,[1] often invoked by earlier classical liberals, as the distinction between authoritative and
non-authoritative intervention. A government activity may
be non-authoritative, and so permissible, if – as with governmental support of scientific research – it imposes no coercive burdens on private initiatives in the areas in which it
operates. The maxim of *laissez faire* may, then, demand simply that the authoritative or coercive activities of government
be restricted to the minimum required for the upholding of
justice, without demanding that government be restricted to
such functions. On this interpretation of *laissez faire*, governmental activity may encompass any manner of service
functions – even including a welfare state – provided these
functions be conducted in a non-coercive fashion.

Like its justice-protecting functions, the service functions
of government are financed from coercive taxation, and it is
on this point that an insoluble problem arises for the theory of
the minimum state. In Nozick's account, which is surely the
best we have available to us, the minimum state exists only to
protect the Lockean rights possessed by men in the state of
nature.[3] Among these rights, in Nozick's variant of the Lockean theory, is an inviolable right to property – a right viol-
ated by taxation of earnings, which Nozick characterizes as
akin to forced labor. How, then, is the minimum state to be
financed? Not by non-coercive means such as user fees or
state lotteries, since, as Nozick himself notes,[3] these would
raise the necessary revenue only if they were monopolies and

so entailed a violation of rights. In fact, as his critics have noted,[4] Nozick's account of the minimum state fails because it contains no theory of taxation. My contention is that this is an unavoidable failure of any Lockean theory of the minimum state – that it cannot account for the necessity of taxation in terms consistent with the inviolability of the basic Lockean rights. The necessary failure of minimum statism is manifest, in Nozick's account, in the proposal that individuals be compensated for the loss of the Lockean state-of-nature right to punish violations of their own rights by the provision of the state's right-protection functions – a proposal that founders on the fact that this transfer of right may not be consented to, and, for those who have not consented, involves an abridgement of rights that within Nozick's theory are treated as infinitely weighty.[5] The failure of Nozick's theory, as of earlier theories such as that of Herbert Spencer in the first edition of *Social Statics*,[6] indicates that the conception of the minimum state is indefensible and, indeed, only partly coherent.

The inadequacy of these Lockean perspectives is a symptom of the inadequacy of the conception of liberal justice as the protection of primordial rights which they express. The most promising alternative approach is one intimated partly in Hayek's work and partly in the Public Choice School. Hayek's work is notable in that, like Rawls (the affinities of whose work to his own Hayek recognizes[7]), Hayek seeks to derive the basic liberal rights from a conception of justice that is procedural in character. The basic rights, in Rawls and in Hayek, are justice-based and not themselves foundational. This is to say that we specify the content of the liberal rights by reflecting on the demands of justice – conceived in Kantian terms by Rawls as encompassing those principles that are chosen in an initial position of fair equality that entrenches the autonomy of the individual, and by Hayek in similarly Kantian though more formal terms of universalizability – rather than by pondering the scope of Lockean rights in an imaginary state of nature. Again, in the somewhat less restrictive version of the contractarian method employed by Buchanan and Tullock,[8] the basic liberal rights arise from the procedure of contract among autonomous individuals (conceived in more Hobbesian fashion) and are not taken to be fundamental moral facts. As against the Lockean approach, which breaks down completely in the domain of taxation, the contractarian approach may yield acceptable principles of fair taxation as part of its general prospect of identifying the constitutional principles of the individualist order.

We need not here inquire in any detail into the question of what principles could be so derived, save to note that any plausible derivation would impose strict limits on governmental powers of taxation. Allowing government complete discretion as to taxation policy clearly collides even with the more permissive interpretation of *laissez faire* outlined in an earlier section, since governments might effectively destroy various initiatives and enterprises (without ever forbidding them) by imposing on them burdensome taxation. For this reason, contemporary classical liberals insist that taxation be according to general rules, uniformly applied, and many of them, such as Hayek and Friedman,[9] have argued that only a system of proportional (as opposed to progressive) taxation is fully consistent with liberal requirements. Proportional taxation would prevent the imposition of redistributive taxation on wealthy or unpopular minorities and would thereby remove a major area of arbitrariness from public policy. Whether or not they advocate proportionality, contemporary classical liberals all advocate that taxation policy be governed by general rules so that governments are prevented in their service activities from curbing economic freedom in subtle and covert ways.

If economic freedom may be undermined by arbitrary taxation, it is no less clear that arbitrary fiscal and monetary policy may similarly injure the economic life of the liberal policy. The recent literature of classical liberalism abounds with proposals for the constitutional regulation of fiscal and monetary policy, designed to avert this arbitrariness, though by no means all contemporary classical liberals are persuaded that the imposition of constitutional rules on governmental activity in these areas is the best antidote to the danger of arbitrary policy. In monetary policy, the chief danger concerning classical liberals has been that of sudden destabilizing fluctuations in the value of money – mostly inflationary over the last four decades, but deflationary in the interwar period – generated by governmental manipulation of the money supply. Led by Milton Friedman, a substantial body of contemporary economic liberals has argued for the control of monetary policy by a fixed rule. Analogously, many contemporary liberals have in the field of fiscal policy advocated a balanced-budget rule compelling the abandonment of deficit financing policy. In these proposals, we see the search for effective constitutional limitations on governmental spending and money-creating activities. Other classical liberals, by contrast, have urged that limiting arbitrary governmental activities in these areas is best achieved by encouraging the growth of countervailing power rather than instituting legal rules which may then be circumvented or altered. In monetary policy, for example, Hayek has urged[10] that depriving government of its monopoly of money-creation is a better way of disciplining its monetary activities than is an attempt on monetarist lines to control them by a fixed rule. Again, advocates of supply-side economic theory[11] resist balanced-budget proposals on the ground that reducing tax levels may actually increase tax revenues by stimulating economic activity, whereas balancing the budget at current tax rates may precipitate recession. I think, however, that these differences are in the end disagreements about transitional strategy rather than about the liberal goal. Hayek certainly favors a monetary constitution that deprives government of its monopoly powers, and the supply-side economists are typically advocates of an automatic gold standard. Common to all contemporary classical liberals is the goal of a form of limited government under the rule of law in which (aside from narrowly demarcated emergency provisions[12]), the central economic powers of government – powers of taxation, spending and the issuance of money – are subject to rules no less stringent than those which protect the basic personal liberties.

It has been remarked in passing that the liberal conception of limited government may even encompass something akin to a welfare state. It is worth stressing that the justification most commonly accepted among contemporary classical liberals for a limited welfare state is not one that endorses the illiberal idea of basic welfare rights, but rather one that appeals to contractarian or utilitarian considerations. In other words, the argument is not that the poor have any right to welfare provision, but rather that such provision may be part of a rational social contract or else may further general welfare. (Some welfare arrangements, including highly redistributive ones, may be justified as rectifying previous violations of liberal justice, as has been observed by Robert Nozick,[13] but this is a possibility that cannot be explored here.) A further point is that many classical liberals have a strong preference for a welfare state whose basic institution is a guaranteed minimum income. The most elegant and economical scheme of this kind is the negative income tax as proposed by Milton Friedman,[14] in which the incomes of the poor are automatically supplemented up to a level of subsistence. Such an arrangement has the virtues, from a liberal standpoint, of minimizing bureaucracy and limiting the danger of paternalism created by welfare schemes which allow a greater measure of discretionary authority to welfare agencies. It also has dangers – the danger that the political competition for votes would force the minimum income up to unrealistic levels and would institutionalize a vast system of outdoor poor relief. For this reason, other contemporary liberals are sceptical of the negative income tax and would prefer a minimal welfare state consisting of safety net services for the poor, preferably provided by local rather than national governments. In general, in social and welfare policy, as elsewhere, the liberal preference is for institutions which restrict liberty to the least practicable extent.

In addition to providing a minimum of welfare services, a liberal state may have certain wholly positive functions as part of the task of maintaining a free order. Among these may be the legislation and enforcement of anti-monopoly regulations, certain consumer protection measures and the inspection of state-funded schools. Such positive tasks for government are regarded with suspicion by many classical liberals, and it may well be that the balance of expediency tells against them. In the field of education and social services, for example, there is much to be said for a system of tax credits and voucher[15] schemes whereby all would be enabled to make private provision for themselves instead of being dependent on uniform and bureaucratic state services. The form of such arrangements cannot be decided *a priori*, but only by reference to specific circumstances. It is the task of liberal policy to devise schemes which discharge the state's service functions without endangering liberty or compromising its general character as a form of limited authority under law.

The conception of the liberal state I have sketched is, in its substance, that of the great classical liberals. It eschews the anarchist tendencies which have so often infected liberal thought with rationalist utopianism and acknowledges the state as a permanent necessary evil. In so doing, it exploits the insight of the Scottish philosophers and Hayek that there is a spontaneous order in social life, but qualifies that insight with the recognition that the spontaneous processes of society can only be beneficial against a background of legal institutions, themselves protected by coercive power, in which the basic liberties are guaranteed for all. The liberal conception of the state eschews no less firmly the revisionary conception of government as the guardian and provider of general welfare. empowered to act on its own discretionary authority in the pursuit of the common good – a conception whose reality is everywhere that of weak government, prey to collusive interest groups and incapable of delivering even the security in enjoyment of basic liberties which is the state's only title to authority.

10

The Attack on Liberalism

Liberalism – and most especially liberalism in its classical form – is the political theory of modernity. Its postulates are the most distinctive features of modern life – the autonomous individual with his concern for liberty and privacy, the growth of wealth and the steady stream of invention and innovation, the machinery of government which is at once indispensable to civil life and a standing threat to it – and its intellectual outlook is one that could have originated in its fullness only in the post-traditional society of Europe after the dissolution of medieval Christendom. Despite its dominance as the political theory of the modern age, liberalism has never been without serious intellectual and political rivals. In their different ways, conservatism and socialism alike are no less responses to the challenges of modernity, whose roots may be traced back to the crises of seventeenth-century England, but which crystallize into definite traditions of thought and practice only in the aftermath of the French Revolution. Both conservative and socialist thinkers suggest genuine criticisms of the liberal outlook and of liberal society which can be understood and addressed only in the historical context in which all three traditions came to birth.

Conservatives have sometimes disdained theoretical reflection on political life, implying that political knowledge is first and last the practical knowledge of a hereditary ruling class as to how affairs of state are to be conducted – a form of knowledge that is best left inarticulate, uncorrupted by rationalist systematizing. The nineteenth and twentieth centuries are nevertheless replete with conservative thought of a sort that is fully as systematic and reflective as any found in the liberal tradition, and rich with insights of which liberal thought can make profitable use. We find in the writings of Hegel, Burke, de Maistre, Savigny, Santayana and Oakeshott – all of them conservatives, if only in sharing a common spirit of reaction against the excesses of liberal rationalism – many incisive criticisms which liberal thought neglects at its peril. Such conservative criticisms are invaluable corrections of the characteristic liberal illusions, but they often embody forms of nostalgia and quixotism which no liberal can support, and they sometimes express clear misconceptions of the character of liberalism itself. So let us consider what it is that distinguishes a conservative view of man and society, and what the conservative view can offer to the liberal.

In its intellectual response to the revolution of 1688 and 1789, conservative thought in England and France, and everywhere thereafter, is distinctive in conceiving the central fact of political life to be the relation of subjects to rulers. For the conservative, relations of authority are aspects of the natural form of social life, not to be accounted for in liberal fashion by any contract among individuals, and still less by reference to moral beliefs of the kind which comprise socialist movements. The stuff of political life is made up of historical communities and is composed of many generations of human beings, shaped by the peculiar traditions of their region and country. Conservative thought proclaims its scepticism of the generic humanity[1] and abstract individuality it sees celebrated in liberalism and insists that the human individual is a cultural achievement rather than a natural fact. As we read it in the works of de Maistre and Burke, conservative thought has as its central terms, authority, loyalty, hierarchy and order – rather than equality, liberty or mankind. The emphasis is on the particularities of political life instead of any universal principles it may be supposed to exemplify. Often, though not always, it is suggested that the role of general ideas in political life is that of an epiphenomenon – a reflection of deeper forces of sentiment, interest and passion. As against liberalism and socialism, then, conservative thought is particularist, and suspicious of the pursuit of equality. It is also sceptical and pessimistic and, in its reaction to the Industrial Revolution, prone to see breakdown and the desolation of old ways and to distrust the opportunities of improvement and liberation wrought by the spread of invention and machinery. Nineteenth-century English conservatism spawned an entire school of historical interpretation and social criticism, which pictured industrialism as bringing about a collapse in popular living standards and disrupting ancient relations of hierarchy in which rulers acknowledged an obligation to the common people. In the political writings of Benjamin Disraeli – perhaps the most influential nineteenth-century English anti-liberal thinker because of his massive political presence, but evincing attitudes shared by many others such as Carlyle, Ruskin and Southey – this hostility to the social implications of the Industrial Revolution generated a nostalgic and fantastic philosophy of Tory paternalism, in which national government performed the duties once discharged by the local nobility.

In many ways socialist thought echoes conservative voices in lamenting the dislocation of ancient folkways brought about by commerce and industry. Friedrich Engels's study of the conditions of the English working class[2] is notable as much for its arcadian representation of pre-industrial life as for its account of contemporary deprivation and misery. Both conservative and socialist writers tend to see in English life, somewhere between the sixteenth century and the nineteenth, a Great Transformation (in Karl Polanyi's terminology[3]) in which communal social forms were shattered by the force of individualism and rising new classes. Unlike conservatives, socialists were for the most part optimists about the social consequences of industrialism and, indeed, regarded the abundance which industry made possible as a necessary condition of progress to the classless egalitarian society. But like conservatives and unlike liberals, socialists mostly repudiated the abstract individualism[4] they found in liberal thought and rejected liberal ideas of civil society in favor of conceptions of moral community. If socialists were always more hopeful than conservatives about the political prospect, in nineteenth-century England and Europe they were at one with conservatives in representing the liberal age as an episode, a transitional phase in social development.

The weaknesses of socialist and conservative thought lie partly in their interpretation of history and partly in the extremely hazy vision of a post-liberal order which their writings contain. Both socialists and conservatives, overreacting to the visible hardships of industrialism, exaggerated its destructive aspects and understated its beneficial impart on the living standards of the people. The early decades of the nineteenth century witnessed a substantial and continuous expansion in population, in the consumption of luxuries and in incomes, which is scarcely to be reconciled with the historical mythology of popular immisertion expressed in Marxist and many conservative writings.[5] Further, at least in the English case, the idea of commerce and industry bringing about a vast rupture in social order seems plainly groundless. As far back as we can go, England was a predominantly individualist society, in which the characteristic institutions of feudalism were weak or absent.[6] Conservative and socialist thinkers and publicists in the nineteenth century seem to have misread the history of the society from which their models of social change were chiefly derived.

It is in their conception of an anti-liberal alternative order that the most radical weakness of socialist and conservative ideas is to be found. By the mid-nineteenth century, individualist patterns of economic and social life had spread over most of Europe (including Russia) and there nowhere remained a traditional social order of unbroken communal ties for conservatives to defend. Where conservatism was a political success – as it was with Disraeli and Bismarck – it achieved this victory by a pragmatic domestication of individualist life and set in motion nothing like the anti-liberal revolution of which Disraeli and other romantic conservatives dreamt. When the liberal order broke down in Europe in 1914, it was replaced over most of the continent by a brutal, farcical and (in Germany) genocidal modernism which cut loose from Western moral and legal traditions and produced a Hobbesian anomie (rather than a reconstitution of communal bonds) whenever its policies were implemented. In turn, twentieth-century history shows no example of a successful anti-liberal conservative movement, and the greatest of conservative statesmen – de Gaulle and Adenauer, for example – have adopted a managerial and realist attitude to modern society which accepts its intractable individualism as an historical fate that wise policy may contain but not reverse.

Socialist hopes of a new form of moral community have fared little better than conservative visions of a renovation of communal life. Expectations of proletarian international solidarity were rudely shattered by the First World War, and the ensuing victory of socialism in an illiberal and revolutionary form in Russia inaugurated a novel political system, but one which had more in common with subsequent National Socialist experiments in totalitarian control than with any socialist ideal. Socialist projects and movements have everywhere come to grief on the stubborn realities of distinctive cultural, national and religious traditions and, beyond them, of the pervasive and ineradicable individualism of modern social life. For all the fashionable socialist rhetoric of alienation, socialist movements have been most enduring and successful when they have sought to temper individualist society rather than to transform it. Just as the only viable form of conservatism appears to be liberal conservatism, so socialism has achieved a measure of success only insofar as it has absorbed the essential elements of liberal civilization.

As offering alternatives to liberal society, conservatism and socialism must be judged failures, yet each provides insights of which the liberal intellectual tradition can make good use. Perhaps the most valuable conservative insight is in its critique of progress – that the advance of knowledge and technology may be deployed as easily for cruel and mad purposes, as in the Holocaust and the Gulag, as for purposes of improvement and liberation. Twentieth-century experience has supported conservative distrust of the belief of the nineteenth-century liberals (a belief that was not shared by the Scottish founders of classical liberalism) that human history manifests a steady trajectory of progress, arrested and sometimes retarded, but irresistible in the end. It is clear now that the only support for the liberal hope comes, not from imagined historical laws or tendencies, but solely from the vitality of liberal civilisation itself. Again, time has proved well-founded conservative suspicions of a mass society whose large numbers are emancipated from the guidance of ancient cultural traditions. The vital truth that the maintenance of moral and cultural traditions is a necessary condition of lasting progress – a truth acknowledged by such liberal thinkers as Tocqueville and Constant, Ortega y Gasset and Hayek – must be accounted a permanent contribution of conservative reflection.

In recent decades, conservative thought has exhibited a diminished hostility to market institutions, and has increasingly come to see in market freedoms a support for the spontaneous order in society which conservatives cherish.[7] By contrast, socialist thought has been slow to come to terms with the indispensability of market institutions, seeing in them symptoms of waste and disorder and a culpable failure of rational planning. There has indeed emerged a school of market socialist thought, owing at least as much to John Stuart Mill as it does to Marx, which conceives the central productive institution of the socialist economy to be the worker cooperative, with resources being allocated among cooperatives by market competitions. In its realistic acceptance of the market's allocative role, the new school of socialist thought represents a welcome departure from conventional socialist confidence in the prospects of central economic planning, but it confronts several hard problems which in combination prove fatal to the market socialist project. There is first the difficulty, noted by the distinguished Keynesian economist J. E. Meade,[8] that breaking up the economy into worker-managed enterprises involves sacrificing important economies of scale. Further, the fusion of job-holding with capital-sharing in the workers cooperative has, as Yugoslav experience demonstrates,[9] the unfortunate consequence of generating unemployment among young workers and encouraging workers in cooperatives to act like family partnerships in slowly consuming capital. If experience is any guide, worker-managed economies are likely to be sluggish, deficient in technological innovation and highly inequitable in the distribution of job opportunities they generate. Finally, all market socialist schemes confront the radical problem of

allocating capital. By what criteria are the central state banks
to allocate capital to the different worker cooperatives? In
market capitalist systems, the provision of venture capital is
recognized as part of entrepreneurship – a creative activity
insusceptible of formulation in hard and fast rules. When the
provision of capital is concentrated in the state, as it is in most
if not all market socialist proposals, what rate of return is to be
demanded, and how is the State Investment Bank to be disciplined for its losses? In any practically realizable form, the
market socialist scheme is open to the crippling objection that
the centralization of capital in government would be bound to
trigger a political competition for resources in which established industries and enterprises would be the winners and
new, risky and weak enterprises the losers. In other words,
market socialism would merely intensify the harmful distributional conflict theorized by public choice analysts[10] in the context of mixed economies.

These defects in market socialist proposals suggest that
there is no feasible alternative to market competition as the
allocative institution for capital, labor and consumer goods in ,
a complex industrial society. The most compelling aspect of
the socialist criticism of economic liberalism lies, accordingly,
not in any aspect of the market mechanism, but in the imperfections from the standpoint of justice of the initial allocation
of resources. All real societies present a distribution of capital
and income which results from many factors, including previous acts of injustice in the form of violations of property
rights, restrictions on contractual liberty, and inequitable
uses of economic power. It is for this reason that Robert
Nozick has proposed[11] the adoption of John Rawls's Difference Principle as a rule of thumb for the rectification of past
injustices. In all likelihood, Nozick goes too far in recom-
mending a stringent egalitarian principle for the redistribution of income as a rectificatory response to the historic burden of past injustices, and there is no justification for attempting to bring about any pattern of income or wealth distribution. The aim of policy ought not to be the imposition of any
such pattern, since respect for liberty dictates acceptance of
the disruption of patterns by free choices, but instead to compensate for past departures from equal liberty. This is not best

achieved by an egalitarian policy of income redistribution.

A more appropriate response to the reality of injustice in the distribution of capital is a redistribution of capital itself, perhaps in the form of a negative capital tax[12] which would supply the propertyless with a patrimony of wealth which would compensate them for the effects of previous injustices. It would be a virtue of such a redistributional policy, from a classical liberal viewpoint, if it could be financed by the sale of state assets and so need not entail further governmental encroachment on private capital. Whether or not this proposal be accepted as practicable, it is a valid insight of socialist thought, and one recognized most fully by the theorists of the Public Choice School, that a restoration of economic freedom presupposes in justice a redistribution of capital holdings.

Conservative and socialist attacks on liberalism have a vital role in alerting us to the shortcomings of liberal thought and society. Above all, they should help us resist the temptation to suppose that liberal society is ever to be identified with its contingent historical forms. If conservative reflection teaches us to be cautious in our attitude to our inheritance of moral and cultural traditions, socialist thought compels recognition of the truth that the moral defense of liberty requires rectification of past injustices by a renegotiation of established rights. The defense of liberal society requires, in short, that liberal thought and practice be ready to adopt conservative and radical perspectives when these may be demanded by liberal goals and by the historical circumstance in which liberal societies find themselves.

The Conclusion:
Liberalism and the
Future

Liberalism is that principle of political rights, according to
which the public authority, in spite of being all-powerful,
limits itself and attempts, even at its own expense, to leave
room in the State over which it rules for those to live who
neither think nor feel as it does, that is to say as do the stronger
majority. Liberalism – it is well to recall this today – is the
supreme form of generosity; it is the right which the majority
concedes to minorities and hence it is the noblest cry that has
ever resounded on this planet. It announces the determination
to share existence with the enemy; more than that, with an
enemy which is weak. It was incredible that the human species
should have arrived at so noble an attitude, so paradoxical, so
refined, so anti-natural. Hence it is not to be wondered at that
this same humanity should soon appear anxious to get rid of it.
It is a discipline too difficult and complex to take firm root
on earth. (Jose Ortega y Gasset, *The Revolt of the Masses*,
London, 1932, p. 83.)

Throughout this study I have represented liberalism as the
political theory of modernity. For all its anticipations in the
ancient world, the liberal outlook is a creature of modernity in
that it presupposes the cultural achievements – the morality of
individuality and a diversity of forms of life in society – by
which the modern world is best distinguished. In fact,
liberalism is perhaps most fully understood when it is
conceived as the response of modern men to an historical

circumstance in which, because the traditional social order has passed away, the powers and limits of governments need redefinition. From this perspective, liberalism is a search for principles of political justice that will command rational assent among persons with different conceptions of the good life and different views of the world. The conception of human nature which liberalism expresses is, in the end, a distillation of the modern experience of variety and conflict in moral life: it is the conception of man as a being with the moral capacity of forming a conception of the good life and the intellectual capacity of articulating that conception in a systematic form.

As it is given us in the classical liberalism of the Scottish philosophers, this conception of man as a rational and moral being is not associated with a doctrine of human perfectibility and it does not issue in any expectation that men will converge upon a single, shared view of the ends of life. Rather, the hope of the classical liberals was the humbler one that, in a political order which respected and protected the diversity in thought and practice which we find among us, we might learn from one another and achieve an alleviation of the human lot by the peaceful competition of different traditions. The classical liberal advocacy of the free market is, in effect, only an application in the sphere of economic life of the conviction that human society is likely to do best when men are left free to enact their plans of life unconstrained except by the rule of law. Just as in the market process enterprises will be sifted out which do not respond to changing circumstances, so in the larger life of society, the classical liberals believed, we will benefit from a continuing antagonism of ideas and proposals. Even when they harbored dark doubts as to the ultimate stability of free societies, the classical liberals remained convinced that our best hope of progress lies in releasing the spontaneous forces of society to develop in new, unthought of and sometimes conflicting directions. For them, progress consisted not in the imposition on society of any rational plan, but rather in the many unpredictable forms of growth and advance which occur when human efforts are not bound by prevailing conceptions to follow a common direction.

One contrast on which my account of liberalism has turned

is the contrast between classical and modern liberalism. We can now see that the decisive break in the liberal intellectual tradition came, not with the abandonment of natural rights theory for Utilitarianism or the replacement of a negative conception of liberty with a positive one, but instead with a new and hubristic rationalism. Whereas the classical liberals of the Scottish school, like the great French liberals Constant and Tocqueville, had seen a primary argument for liberty in the incapacity of human intelligence to grasp the society that had produced it, the new liberals sought to submit the life of society to rational reconstruction. If, for the classical liberals, progress is, so to speak, an emergent property of free exchanges among men, for the modern liberals progress becomes the realization in the world of a specific conception of the rational society. This is seen clearly in the work of John Stuart Mill, a divided and ambiguous thinker whose orientation nevertheless lies in the last resort with the modern liberals. Once progress is conceived as the realization of a rational plan of life rather than as the unpredictable exfoliation of human energies, it is inevitable that liberty should eventually be subordinated to the claims of progress. This is a conflict which the classical liberals avoided with their wise admission that human intelligence cannot plot the course of the future. We are better employed in devising a framework in which we may make our own trials and errors than in attempting to force on all a preferred path to improvement.

With the decline of the classical liberal system of thought, liberalism assumed its modern form, in which rationalistic intellectual hubris is fused with a sentimental religion of humanity. The decline of the classical system of liberal thought coincided with, and was in very significant measure occasioned by, the arrival of a mass democracy in which the constitutional order of the free society soon came to be alterable by the processes of political competition. Liberal thought quickly endorsed the new conception of the rule of government engendered by the struggle for votes in a mass democracy – the conception of government as the provider of general welfare and not, as hitherto, the guardian of the framework within which individuals may provide for themselves. Long before its collapse in 1914, a radical instability had entered into the liberal order as the pressures of political competition began slowly to transform the institutions of limited government into those of a totalitarian democracy. Across the continent of Europe, liberal institutions were everywhere shaken in the aftermath of the Great War, and by the 1930s everything appeared to support Ortega's hard saying that liberty was a burden that mankind was only too anxious to throw off.

Half a century later, it is still too early to know if Ortega was justified in expressing a pessimism he shared with other despairing liberals such as Max Weber and Vilfredo Pareto. But there are many signs that liberals ideas and institutions are regaining a hold on men's loyalties. Now that the vast promises of the new liberalism have been widely perceived to be spurious, thought is returning to the insights of the older liberals, and their applications are being worked out in many areas of policy. As it has been newly stated in the works of Hayek, Buchanan and others, the old liberalism embodies a radical critique of the dominant habits of thought and action of our time. The new classical liberals develop an incisive criticism of the unlimited popular democracy by which we are in effect ruled, and of the rationalist philosophy which supports the interventionist state in its attempts at social engineering. The restoration of a liberal order of basic liberties under law, if it is possible at all, cannot be an easy matter, since it demands something akin to a constitutional revolution – a radical reform of political institutions which, to be successful, must be preceded by an intellectual revolution in which current modes of thought are discarded. No one can predict the outcome of the current revival of liberal thought. But, if there is hope for the future of liberty, it is in the fact that, as we approach the end of a century of political frenzy, we see a return to the wisdom of the great liberal writers. For it is in the works of the classical liberal thinkers that we have the most profound reflective response to the dangers and opportunities of the modern age.

Notes

Chapter 1

1. G. B. Kerferd, *The Sophistic Movement,* Cambridge: Cambridge University Press, 1981, p. 144.
2. E. A. Havelock, *The Liberal Temper in Greek Politics,* New Haven: Yale University Press, 1957.
3. K. R. Popper, *The Open Society and Its Enemies,* London: Routledge and Kegan Paul, 1945.
4. Alasdair MacIntyre, *After Virtue: A study in moral theory,* London: Duckworth and Co., 1981, p. 67.
5. On this, see Leo Strauss, *Natural Right and History,* Chicago: University of Chicago Press, 1953.
6. I owe this point to Neera Badhwar.
7. F. A. Hayek, *The Constitution of Liberty,* London: Routledge and Kegan Paul, 1960, p. 166.

Chapter 2

1. Leo Strauss, 'On the Spirit of Hobbes's Political Philosophy', in K. C. Brown, ed., *Hobbes Studies,* Oxford: Basil Blackwell, 1965, p. 13.
2. Michael Oakeshott, *Hobbes on Civil Association,* Oxford: Basil Blackwell, 1975, p. 63.
3. C. B. Macpherson, *The Political Theory of Possessive Individualism,* Oxford: Clarendon Press, 1962.
4. Stuart Hampshire, *Two Theories of Morality,* Oxford: Oxford University Press, p. 56.
5. See Peter Laslett's edition of John Locke, *Two Treatises of Government,* Cambridge: Cambridge University Press, 1967.
6. Alan Macfarlane, *The Origins of English Individualism: The family, property and social transition,* Cambridge: Cambridge University Press, 1978.
7. John Dunn, *The Political Thought of John Locke,* Cambridge: Cambridge University Press, 1969.
8. On this, see the seminal study by James Tully, *A Discourse of Property: John Locke and his Adversaries,* New York: Cambridge University Press, 1980.

9. See Tully, op. cit.
10. W. H. Greenleaf, *Order, Empiricism and Politics: Two traditions of English political thought,* 1500–1700, Westport, Conn.: Greenwood Press, 1980, p. 265; and W. H. Greenleaf, *The British Political Tradition,* vol. 2: *The ideological heritage,* London: Methuen, 1983, p. 22.
11. G. de Ruggiero, *The History of European Liberalism,* Oxford: Oxford University Press, 1927, p. 24.
12. On this, see Ruggiero, op. cit., pp. 395–406.

Chapter 3

1. Marquis de Condorcet, The History of Human Progress, Book Ten, as revised by Nicholas Capaldi, *The Enlightenment: The Proper Study of Mankind,* New York: G. P. Putnam's Sons, 1965, p. 312.
2. Benjamin Constant, 'Liberty Ancient and Modern', as quoted in G. de Ruggiero, *The History of European Liberalism,* Oxford: Oxford University Press, 1927, pp. 167–168.
3. D. G. Ritchie, *Natural Rights,* London: Allen and Unwin, 1894, p. 3.

Chapter 4

1. A. J. P. Taylor, *English History 1914–1945,* Oxford: Oxford University Press, 1965, p. 1.
2. G. J. Goschen, *Laissez-faire and Government Interference,* London, 1883, p. 3, as quoted in W. H. Greenleaf, *The British Political Tradition,* vol. 2: *The ideological heritage,* London: Methuen, 1983, p. 44.
3. On Disraeli, see Isaiah Berlin's beautiful psychological study, 'Benjamin Disraeli, Karl Marx and the Search for Identity', in I. Berlin, *Against the Current,* London: Hogarth Press, 1980, pp. 262–286.
4. A. V. Dicey, *Lectures on the Relation between Law and Public Opinion in England during the Nineteenth Century,* 1905, p. 432, as quoted in Greenleaf, op. cit., p. 105.
5. L. T. Hobhouse, *Liberalism,* 1911, repr. 1966, p. 58, as quoted in Greenleaf, op. cit., vol. II, p. 103.
6. Greenleaf, op. cit., p. 49.
7. See, especially, Henry Sidgwick, 'The Relations of Ethics with Sociology', in *Miscellaneous Essays and Addresses,* London: Macmillan, 1904.
8. Norman Stone, *Europe Transformed 1878–1919,* Cambridge, Mass.: Harvard University Press, 1984, p. 201.
9. A. J. P. Taylor, *English History 1914–1945,* Oxford: Oxford University Press, 1965, p. 2.
10. See Sir Ernest Benn, *Happier Days: Recollections and Reflections,* London, 1949.

Chapter 5

1. On Berlin's value-pluralist defense of individual liberty, see my 'On Negative and Positive Liberty', in Z. A. Pelczynski and John Gray, eds, *Conceptions of Liberty in Political Philosophy,* London: Athlone Press, and St. Martin's Press, New York, 1984.
2. See John Gray, *Hayek on Liberty,* Oxford: Basil Blackwell, 1984, Chapter One, for a discussion of the delayed reception of Hayek's work.
3. See Murray N. Rothbard, *America's Great Depression,* New York: Richardson, 1983.
4. See Rothbard, passim.
5. See F. A. Hayek, *Studies in Philosophy, Politics and Economics,* London: Routledge and Kegan Paul, 1967, p. 194.
6. For a powerful criticism of the failure of 'free market conservatism' to defend personal liberties, see Samuel Brittan, *Capitalism and the Permissive Society,* London: Macmillan, 1973.
7. James Buchanan, *Freedom in Constitutional Contract,* College Station, Texas: Texas A & M University Press, 1977; and James Buchanan, *Limits of Liberty: Between Anarchy and Leviathan,* Chicago: Chicago University Press, 1975.

Chapter 6

1. Alasdair MacIntyre, *After Virtue: A study in moral theory,* London: Duckworth and Co., 1981, p. 204.
2. Bernard Williams, *Morality: An Introduction to Ethics,* New York: Harper and Row, 1972, pp. 64–65.
3. Stuart Hampshire, *Freedom of Mind,* Princeton, N.J.: Princeton University Press, 1971, pp. 78–79.
4. See Hillel Steiner, 'The Structure of a Set of Compossible Rights', *Journal of Philosophy,* **LXXIV** (12), Dec. 1977, pp. 767–775.
5. See Stuart Hampshire, 'Morality and Pessimism', as reprinted in Hampshire's *Morality and Conflict,* Oxford: Basil Blackwell, 1983; and H. L. A. Hart, *The Concept of Law,* Oxford, Clarendon Press, 1961, pp. .
6. John Gray, *Mill on Liberty: A defence,* London: Routledge and Kegan Paul, 1983.
7. John Rawls, *A Theory of Justice,* Cambridge, Mass.: Belnap Press of the Harvard University Press, 1971.
8. See, most particularly, James Buchanan's *Freedom in Constitutional Contract,* College Station, Texas: Texas A & M University Press, 1977.
9. David Gauthier, *Morals by Agreement,* Oxford: Oxford University Press, 1985.

Chapter 7

1. Isaiah Berlin, 'Two Concepts of Liberty', in *Four Essays on Liberty,* Oxford: Oxford University Press, 1969.
2. F. A. Hayek, *The Constitution of Liberty,* London: Routledge and Kegan Paul, 1960, pp. 16–17.
3. For an account of freedom as the non-restriction of options, see S. I. Benn and W. L. Weinstein, 'Being Free to Act and Being a Free Man', *Mind,* **80**, 1971, pp. 194–211.
4. See I. Berlin, op. cit. pp. 145–154.
5. See F. A. Hayek, op. cit., pp. 146–147.
6. Especially in his reviews of Tocqueville's *Democracy in America* and the essay on 'The Spirit of the Age'.
7. See John Rawls, *A Theory of Justice,* Oxford: Oxford University Press, 1971, pp. 201–205.
8. I am indebted here to Joel Feinberg's formulation in J. Feinberg, *Social Philosophy,* Englewood Cliffs, N.J.: Prentice-Hall Inc., 1973, pp.15–16.

Chapter 8

1. Robert Nozick, *Anarchy, State and Utopia,* New York: Basic Books, 1974, pp. .
2. See A. M. Honore, 'Social Justice', in R. S. Summers, ed., *Essays in Legal Philosophy,* Oxford: Clarendon Press, 1968.
3. I have discussed the idea of practical knowledge in my *Hayek on Liberty,* Oxford: Basil Blackwell, 1984, pp. 14–15.
4. See Hayek, *The Constitution of Liberty,* Chicago: Henry Regnery, 1960, p. 121.
5. Hayek, op. cit., ch. 21.
6. Hayek, op. cit., p. 126.
7. Michael Oakeshott, *Rationalism in Politics,* London: Methuen, 1962, p. 46.
8. Leon Trotsky, *The Revolution Betrayed,* New York: 1937, p. 76.
9. Robert Nozick, *Anarchy, State and Utopia,* New York: Basic Books, 1974, p. 321.
10. F. A. Hayek, *Studies in Philosophy, Politics and Economics,* London: Routledge and Kegan Paul, 1967, pp. 164–165.
11. On the 'calculation debate', see Dan C. Lavoie, *Rivalry and Central Planning: The socialist calculation debate reconsidered,* Cambridge: Cambridge University Press, 1985.
12. See Murray N. Rothbard, *America's Great Depression,* New York: Richardson, 1983; and Milton Friedman, *The Great Contraction* (with Anna Schwartz), Princeton, N.J.: Princeton University Press, 1965.
13. See G. L. S. Shackle, *Epistemics and Economics,* Cambridge: Cambridge University Press, 1976, p. 239.
14. J. Schumpeter, *Capitalism, Socialism and Democracy,* London: Unwin University Books, 1943, pp. 81–87.

Chapter 9

1. See on this my *Mill on Liberty: A defence,* London: Routledge and Kegan Paul, pp. 60–63.
2. Robert Nozick, *Anarchy, State, and Utopia,* New York: Basic Books, 1974, ch. 5.
3. Nozick, op. cit., p. 25.
4. See Murray N. Rothbard, *The Ethics of Liberty,* Atlantic Highlands, N.J.: Humanities Press, 1982, ch. 29.
5. But see Nozick, op. cit., p. 30, footnote.
6. Herbert Spencer, *Social Statics,* New York: Robert Schalkenbach Foundation, 1970, ch. XIX.
7. F. A. Hayek, *Law, Legislation and Liberty,* vol. 2: *The mirage of social justice,* Chicago: University of Chicago Press, 1976, p. xiii.
8. See James Buchanan and Gordon Tullock, *The Calculus of Consent,* Michigan: University of Michigan Press, 1962.
9. See Hayek, *The Constitution of Liberty,* Chicago: Henry Regnery, 1960, ch. 20; and Milton Friedman, *Capitalism and Freedom,* Chicago: Chicago University Press, 1962, pp. 174–175.
10. See F. A. Hayek, *The Denationalisation of Money,* 2nd Edition, London: Institute of Economic Affairs, 1978.
11. For a statement of supply-side economic theory, see George Gilder, *Wealth and Poverty,* New York: Basic Books, 1981.
12. On constitutional provisions for emergency, see F. A. Hayek, *Law, Legislation and Liberty,* vol. 3: *The political order of a free people,* London: Routledge and Kegan Paul, 1979, pp. 124–126.
13. Nozick, op. cit., pp. 230–231.
14. Milton Friedman, *Capitalism and Freedom,* Chicago: University of Chicago Press, 1962, pp. 190–193.
15. Friedman, op. cit., pp. 89–90.

Chapter 10

1. For an insightful criticism of the liberal notion of generic humanity, see K. R. Minogue, *The Liberal Mind,* New York: Vintage Books, 1968, pp. 52–61.
2. F. Engels, *The Condition of the Working Class in England,* New York: J. W. Lovell Company, 1887.
3. Karl Polanyi, *The Great Transformation,* Boston: Beacon Press, 1957.
4. For a criticism of the liberal idea of the abstract individual, see Steven Lukes, *Individualism,* Oxford: Basil Blackwell, 1973.
5. On popular living standards during the Industrial Revolution, see R. M. Hartwell, *The Industrial Revolution and Economic Growth,* London: Methuen, 1971.
6. See on this, Alan MacFarlane, *The Origins of English Individualism: The family, property and social transition,* Cambridge: Cambridge University Press, 1978.

7. For a conservative endorsement of market institutions, see Lord Coleraine, *For Conservatives Only,* London: Tom Stacey, 1970.
8. See J. E. Meade, *The Intelligent Radical's Guide to Economic Policies,* London: G. Allen and Unwin, 1975.
9. See J. Dorn, 'Markets, True and False: The case of Yugoslavia', *Journal of Libertarian Studies,* 2 (3), Fall 1978, pp. 243–268.
10. See James Buchanan and Gordon Tullock, *The Calculus of Consent,* Michigan: University of Michigan Press, 1962.
11. Robert Nozick, *Anarchy, State, and Utopia,* New York: Basic Books, 1974, pp. 230–231.
12. For a proposal for a negative capital tax, see A. B. Atkinson, *Unequal Shares,* Harmondsworth: Penguin Books, 1972, p. 232.

Bibliography

The classic study of liberalism remains that of G. de Ruggiero, *Storia des liberalismo europea*, Bari, 1925, translated by R. G. Collingwood as *The History of European Liberalism*, Oxford, 1927, which contains a most useful bibliography of earlier works. E. Halevy's *The Growth of Philosophic Radicalism*, London, 1928, gives a masterly account of the transition from the Scottish School to modern British liberalism.

The following list gives in chronological order some of the better later works on liberalism.

Ritchie, D. G., *Natural Rights*, London, 1894; reprinted, 1924.

Hobhouse, L. T., *Liberalism*, London, 1911.

Martin, B. Kingsley, *French Liberal Thought in the Eighteenth Century*, London, 1926; new ed. 1954.

Mises, L. von, *Liberalismus*, Jena, 1927.

Croce,B., *Etica e Politica*, Bari, 1931.

Laski, H., *The Rise of European Liberalism*, London, 1931.

Pohlenz, M., *Die griechische Freiheit*, Heidelberg, 1935; trans. as *The Idea of Freedom in Greek Life and Thought*, Dordrecht, 1963.

Lippmann, W., *An Inquiry into the Principles of Good Society*, Boston and London, 1937.

Sabine, G. H., *A History of Political Theory*, New York, 1937.

McIlwain, C. H., *Constitutionalism and the Changing World*, New York, 1939.

Hallowell, J. H., *The Decline of Liberalism as an Ideology*, Berkeley, California, 1943.

Slesser, H., *A History of the Liberal Party*, London, 1943.

Roepke, W., *Civitas Humana*, Zurich, 1944.

Diez del Corral, L., *El Liberalismo doctrinario*, Madrid, 1945.

Popper, K. R., *The Open Society and Its Enemies*, London, 1945.

Rustow, A., *Das Versagen des Wirtschaftsliberalismus als religionssoziologisches Problem*, Zurich, 1945.

Federici, F., *Der Deutsche Liberalismus*, Zurich, 1946.

Watkins, F., *The Political Tradition of the West*, Cambridge, Mass., 1948.

Wormuth, F. D., *The Origin of Modern Constitutionalism*, New York, 1949.

Polanyi, M., *The Logic of Liberty*, London, 1951.

Eucken, W., *Grundsatze der Wirtschaftpolitik*, Tubingen, 1952.

Robbins, L. C., *The Theory of Economic Policy in English Classical Political Economy*, London, 1952.

Talmon, J. L., *The Origins of Totalitarianism Democracy*, London, 1952.

Cranston, M., *Freedom*, London, 1953.

Lubtow, U. von, *Blute und Verfall der romischen Freiheit*, Berlin, 1953.

Neill, T. P., *Rise and Decline of Liberalism*, Milwaukee, Wisconsin, 1953.

Thomas, R. H., *Liberalism, Nationalism and the German Intellectuals*, Chester Springs, Pa., 1953.

Mayer-Maly, T., 'Rechtsgeschichte der Freiheitsidee in Antike und Mittelalter', *Osterreichische Zeitschaft fur offentliches Recht*, N.F. **VI**, 1954.

Hartz, L., *The Liberal Tradition in America*, New York, 1955.

Bullock, A. and Shock, M., *The Liberal Tradition from Fox to Keynes*, London, 1956.

Wirszubski, C., *Liberties as a Political Ideal at Rome*, Cambridge, 1956.

Havelock, E. A., *The Liberal Temper in Greek Politics*, New Haven, 1957.

Feuer, L. S., *Spinoza and the Rise of Liberalism*, Boston, 1958.

Grifo, G., 'Su alcuni aspetti della liberta in Roma', *Archivoi Giuridico 'Filippo Serafini*, **6** (XXIII), 1958.

Grampp, W. D., *The Manchester School of Economics*, Stanford, California, 1960.

Hayek, F. A. *The Constitution of Liberty*, London and Chicago, 1960.

Friedmann, M., *Capitalism and Freedom*, Chicago, 1962.

Macpherson, C. B., *The Political Theory of Possessive Individualism: Hobbes to Locke*, Oxford, 1962.

Girvetz, H. K., *The Evolution of Liberalism*, New York, 1963.

Schapiro, J. S., *Condorcet and the Rise of Liberalism*, New York, 1963.

Wheeler, *The Rise and Fall of Liberal Democracy*, Santa Barbara, Cal., 1953.

Grampp, W. D., *Economic Liberalism*, New York, 1965.

Bohm, F., 'Privatrechtsgesellschaft und Marktwirtschaft', in *Ordo*, **XVII**, 1966.

Lucas, J. R., *Principles of Politics*, Oxford, 1966.

Vincent, John, *The Formation of the Liberal Party 1857–1868*, London, 1966.

Selinger, M., *The Liberal Politics of John Locke*, London, 1968.

Rawls, John, *A Theory of Justice*, Cambridge, Mass., 1971.

Cumming, R. D., *Human Nature and History, A Study of the Development of Liberal Thought*, Chicago, 1971.

Douglas, R., *The History of the Liberal Party 1890–1970*, London, 1971.

Hamer, D. A., *Liberal Politics in the Age of Gladstone and Rosebery*, Oxford, 1972.

Nozick, John, *Anarchy, State and Utopia*, New York, 1974.

Manning, David, *Liberalism*, London, 1976.

Macfarlane, Alan, *Origins of English Individualism*, Oxford, 1978.

Index

Index